TA/31

S0-BRB-964

J. M. HODGES LEARNING CENTER
WHARTON COUNTY JUNIOR COLLEGE
WHARTON, TEXAS 77488

HOW TO ORGANIZE
AND COACH
WINNING BASEBALL

HOW TO ORGANIZE

AND COACH

WINNING BASEBALL

by Ken Dugan

46778

PARKER PUBLISHING COMPANY, INC.

West Nyack, N.Y.

J. M. HODGES LEARNING CENTER

WHARTON, TEXAS 77488

© 1971 by

Parker Publishing Company, Inc.
West Nyack, N.Y.

*All rights reserved. No part of this
book may be reproduced in any form or
by any means, without permission in
writing from the publisher.*

Library of Congress
Catalog Card Number: 71-134895

Second Printing.....June, 1972

Printed in the United States of America
ISBN-0-13- 425637-9
BC

796.357
D878h

46778

DEDICATION

I dedicate this book to my wonderful wife Diane, my daughter Christi, my son Mike and all the young men who played for me at David Lipscomb College.

FOREWORD

In Chapter 11 of this book, *How to Organize and Coach Winning Baseball,* the author says, "So as the Coach builds his club, a great deal of time must be spent in developing"—. The action verbs in the quotation state basic factors in forming a winning baseball team.

I have known the author, Ken Dugan, for eight years. He is a personable, Christian gentleman and a versatile man. He has been coaching baseball since 1960 at David Lipscomb College, Nashville, Tennessee. He is also Director of Athletics and head basketball coach at David Lipscomb. Coach Dugan has created an indoor baseball training program, nationally advertised, which enables him to teach correct baseball techniques. With this program he can become acquainted with each member of the group and work to instill in the individual player the importance of togetherness as a team, and the desire to strive for perfection. He has developed college players to the professional level. The author has written magazine articles for *Scholastic Coach.* Ken Dugan has had a successful coaching career. His record is proof that he ranks as one of the better college coaches.

The author's collection of facts, methods, and fundamentals of baseball has been gathered from research, instruction, and his ten years of experience coaching college baseball. I predict for this book, *How to Organize and Coach Winning Baseball,* a wide circulation and a long period of usefulness.

Kerby Farrell
Coach, Cleveland Indians

PLAY BALL

The purpose of this book is to provide baseball coaches with comprehensive instructional material including the guiding principles for all aspects of the game. Although planned especially for the high school and college coach, it meets the needs for all age groups from the little league through the college coaching course. The aim constantly in mind throughout its preparation has been to aid all coaches in developing the abilities of their players and to make them more keenly aware of the personal qualities and insight necessary for success.

The coach who carefully studies this book and supplements it with practice and personal instruction should acquire a thorough understanding of the techniques of the game. By reviewing the materials, he will increase his ability to judge players' skills and his information concerning game strategy. He will find valuable teaching tips, methods for conducting tryouts and practice drills, strategy aids, and a system for developing a winning team. He will learn how to secure the most efficient results from batting practice, how to take infield properly, how to teach young players to throw correctly, how to deal with problems of staleness, what can be done on the bench to help the team, and why charts and records are a necessity for a successful coach.

No attempt is made to include all the techniques of baseball but rather to stress the latest and most successful methods of coaching and playing. The book is the compiled knowledge of many professional players and men who now are coaching. An attempt is made to answer questions which have been in coaches' minds for a long time, to present a kind of "baseball bible" that can be used in the classroom or on the playing field to solve problems confronting the coach.

Some of the unique features of the book are a section on batting faults and how to correct them, a section on hitting the curve ball, a section on batting slumps, and discussions of batters' weaknesses and how to pitch to them, the correct way for a run-down and pick-off plays that will work, the squeeze play and how to make it effective, training in the gym, developing skills in the gym during unfavorable weather, and the neglected subject of base-running.

Other features are the chapters on General Offensive Play, which covers offensive situations and strategy, and Defensive Plays and Strategy, which discusses team defense, cut-off plays, relays, bunt situation, and defensing the delayed and double steal.

Completing this coaching tool are game winning tips on such topics as selecting the most potent batting order, determining the defensive line-up, pitching readiness, mental aspects of hitting, placement of bunts, training first and third base coaches, giving signals, and teaching outfielders to get a good jump on fly balls. Other new techniques and methods are noted in discussions of each position on defense and all the fine arts of offense. These features added to the presentation of the basic principles make this a complete baseball guidebook.

Ken Dugan

ACKNOWLEDGEMENTS

The author would like to acknowledge the many people who have helped make this book possible:

To Herman Masin, editor of *Scholastic Coach,* for his encouragement and assistance in initiating this book;

To Dr. Lewis Maiden and Dr. Leota Maiden for their invaluable help in preparing the manuscript;

To Miss Diane Beasley for typing the manuscript;

To President Athens Clay Pullias, Vice President Willard Collins and Dean Mack Wayne Craig of David Lipscomb College for their invaluable advice and encouragement;

To Dave Hall, coach, Columbia State College, Jim Turner, New York Yankee Pitching Coach, Robert Montgomery, Boston Red Sox, and Don Mincher, Oakland Athletics for reading parts of the manuscript and offering many helpful suggestions;

To the many fine friends and coaches with whom the author has been associated while coaching the game: George Leonard, sports writer, *Nashville Banner;* Wes Livengood, scout, Philadelphia Phillies; Kerby Farrell, coach, Cleveland Indians; Buddy Lewis, scout, St. Louis Cardinals; Coach Jim Pickins, Western Kentucky State University; Coach Al Brown, Memphis State Universtiy; Coach Gary Davis, David Lipscomb College; Coach Harold Pickel, Birmingham Southern College; Roy Pardue, Nashville, Tennessee

The contents of this book includes many ideas of these people and others with whom the author has been associated while playing and coaching.

CONTENTS

Part I

GENERAL TEAM AND FIELD MANAGEMENT

1

THE COACH AND
TEAM ORGANIZATION

The baseball coach must esteem his profession as noble and honorable. In the average community, he is a respected individual. Since his conduct will be regarded as an expression of the ideals of his vocation, he should never cast unfavorable reflections upon it. As he comes in daily contact with numerous people, his every act or word may create a multitude of varying impressions. He will never make disparaging comments about a fellow coach or downgrade his work. He will regard as successful, those coaches who work hard, organize efficiently, and possess the ability to develop winning talent. He should remember that self-praise may be discounted as biased, but self-criticism is accepted as frankness. He is a public figure and must live and act accordingly.

Under no circumstances should a coach ever apologize for the choice of his life's work. Pride in the profession is the first requisite for his effectiveness in public relations. To be an outstanding public relationist, he must believe whole heartedly in his vocation and in its importance to the entire educational system.

The coach should demonstrate sound emotional stability in his dealings with his players. He must keep in mind that coaching is teaching, and in the process of teaching, misunderstandings may occur. When they do happen, corrections should be made as soon as possible. There should be a feeling of trust and respect between the coach and his players. They must believe that he is devoted to their baseball welfare. They must always be made welcome in their quest for advice and information. When they come seeking help, it is an indication of their acknowledgment of his leadership. This is the situation that every coach tries to create and which makes coaching pleasurable. This type of communication is bound to result in a successful baseball season.

Team Morale. Morale is a mental state which renders a player capable of endurance and of exhibiting courage in the presence of extreme difficulties. It may be defined further as a person's approach to problems concerned with self-assurance and persistence. This implies that morale is a personal factor, but it involves also an identification of self with some group purpose. For identifying morale in an individual, the term most often used is courage, but in the group, it is spirit. Courage is the carrying out of a course of action in spite of extreme obstacles. Endurance refers to physical and mental lasting powers. It means resistance to fatigue and hurt when circumstances combine to make quitting easier than continuing the struggle.

Therefore, it is the responsibility of the coach to develop a team morale which will give the group a feeling of oneness. To achieve this brand of morale, he must take many factors into consideration. First, he must make a close study of the personnel of his squad and learn each player's ability and disposition. Second, he should attempt to win each player's confidence by dealing fairly and honestly with all members of the team. Third, he must realize that the morale of the baseball team cannot be limited to the players and the coaches. It involves the cooperation of the entire school. The administration and the faculty are very important in the development of this spirit.

The coach must sell not only the players on their own ability, but also the baseball program to the school and the community. The greatest factor in selling is enthusiasm. He must radiate this quality and develop it in each player.

Winning Attitude. There is no substitute for a flaming desire to be a champion. Some players are not willing to pay the price demanded for a champion, and this attitude is the difference between their being good and great or fair and outstanding. They are not willing to come early and stay late or to run that extra lap when it hurts. Some players never know what they can do, because they never push themselves.

It has been the author's experience that each player on a team attaches a different value to winning or losing. The coach should attempt to learn just what each player derives from being a member of the team. Some players will settle for their own success, not caring about the success or failure of the team. The challenge for the coach is to detect the goals of the individual and to see what relationships they have with team success.

Outstanding coaches recognize that they must develop the desire to be a winner. This desire is far more important than the skills and strategies of the game. The coach should possess a deep understanding of the personality of each player on the team. Out of this understanding, he must influence each to adopt the common goal of winning. It must be pointed out here that a coach can defeat his own purpose by intense concentration on winning. Such a coach unsparingly drives his players in an effort to have them approach perfection. Always the coach must bear in mind and convey to his players the concept that perfection is an ideal rather than a reality.

Membership should be fun and pleasure to each member of the squad. Part of this enjoyment should stem from the familiarity existing among the players. Out of this familiarity should come a recognition and appreciation of each other's idiosyncrasies and talents. The locker room may be a stage for camaraderie, which should develop harmonious rapport among the players. Nicknames which are complimentary are valuable. They show the individual that a particular ability is recognized and appreciated. If the team has not given names to members of the squad, it may pay dividends for the coach to find complimentary nicknames for every player. Individuals who can appreciate each other will find it easier to perform as a closely knit unit during the game.

Team Discipline. Discipline, the guidance and control of behavior, is a by-product of good coaching. Its goal is self-discipline by the player as a result of positive motivation. It is a relationship established by the coach which draws from players the type of response that leads to successful performance on the field. To effect this attitude, the coach must use a basic tool of discipline—good organization. Players respect a coach who comes to the field with evidence that he knows "his stuff." He has a schedule of practice which insures the systematic progress of all players engaged.

The observing of training rules is a must for team morale and discipline. If a member of the team disregards the rules and is not punished when caught, the morale of the team and respect for the coach decrease. Serious disciplinary problems should be handled in private. This immediately places the coach in a position of being a dictator, lawmaker, accuser, prosecutor, and judge. There is no higher appeal. However, he should never abuse this power, or he will lose a player's respect.

Discipline on the field will manifest itself in self-control later in life. This transfer is made possible because the moment a player yields to his impulses, he gives up his right to play. Self-control requires courage. There is nothing more disconcerting than a player who is not his own master. During a close game when the going is tough and players are prone to anger, only the well-disciplined will obey the rules. Good discipline practiced every day enables players to keep a grip upon themselves regardless of pressure.

The moment a player receives his uniform, he becomes a member of a select group. He can take pride in being a part of something special. With this privilege, he must realize, belongs the responsibility for conduct and appearance on and off the field. He must look and act like a gentleman, worthy of representing his school and its team.

One of the chief concerns of a coach is the establishment of a spirit of teamwork and togetherness among the team members. This is absolutely essential for a team to be successful in its level of play. Teamwork implies a cooperative attitude toward a cooperative endeavor. Togetherness implies that the team members associate with each other as much as possible. It is helpful for them to date together, study together, eat together, and play together.

The Bench. Many coaches overlook the bench as a factor in building a winning team. If good discipline and team morale are to be achieved, these players must feel they are a member of the squad. In many cases the reserve players are as valuable as some of the men on the playing field. Baseball is a team game, and this means every man in uniform. Everyone on the squad when not on the field should be seated on the bench and be a participant in the ball game at all times—mentally and spiritually. There should be no visiting with friends and parents during the game; this can be done when it is ended.

An alert bench reflects good coaching, the kind that insists on attention to detail and instills in every squad member the belief that he is an integral part of a successful organization. He may uncover valuable information about the opponents that will help his team. The bench at Lipscomb on numerous occasions have detected the opponent's signals, pitching faults, and failure to tag bases.

The bench can lend vocal encouragement to the men on the field and help them when possible by shouting instructions to a player pursuing a fly ball nearby. They can help the catcher also when a runner is stealing by shouting, "There he goes." In addition, they may be used to keep charts, records and notes which can be very valuable to the coach. But above all, the players on the bench should gear themselves for the time they may actually take part in the game.

Conducting Try-Outs. Each year at Lipscomb "try-outs" are conducted during the fall baseball program. By the fall program, each new prospect will have a better opportunity to display his skills. There is no pressure to prepare for scheduled games, and the weather usually is ideal at this time of year. The prospects have played ball all summer, and they are in excellent physical condition to perform on the field. The fall practice may last several weeks with games being played every Saturday. When fall practice has concluded, the coach has his squad chosen and a smaller group to work with the following spring. This also is an excellent time for returning lettermen to work on their weaknesses. If the facilities are available, the fall baseball program is recommended.

Regardless of when a new group of prespects are "trying-out," there are certain rules and procedures to follow. Even though the selection of players is based mostly on subjective judgment, the coach should be impartial and deliberate in making decisions concerning them. He may be mistaken about a player's ability, but that player must feel he has had an opportunity to show his talents. If this is not done, the coach is hurting his program in the school.

In picking the team, both the offensive and defensive abilities of each player must be considered. For example, a good hitter may be a poor defensive player and of less value to the team than another player who does not hit as well but plays much better defense. It should also be mentioned that some players are routine in practice but outstanding in game situations. For this reason practice games are recommended. Another factor a coach should consider in selecting his team is the player's attitude toward his school work. A player with low grades is likely to be one who will have trouble remaining eligible. Good grades, good study habits, and proper attitude toward school work go hand in hand with the potential athletic ability of the player. It is difficult to discipline one's self in one area and not be the same type of individual in another. The player always having trouble in school will sooner or later hurt the team. The best student is usually the best athlete.

The length of "try-outs" will vary with the circumstances, such as the number of coaches, the number of people trying out, the facilities, and the length of practice time. It is important for the coach to have some type of check-list to evaluate each individual. Remembering the names of all the new prospects and the judgments made concerning their abilities will be difficult. Some coaches use numbers to evaluate the player's skills. Each skill will receive a number ranging from one through ten, the higher the number the greater the skill. The coach must make a complete list of skills to be evaluated which are meaningful to him.

As "try-outs" are being conducted and players rated, he should keep in mind the desired qualities for each positon. Some players play one position when they would be more effective in another. Each player should be given a chance at his first choice, but the coach should not hesitate to move him to another position to help the team.

The Batting Order. From the offensive standpoint, all players on a team rarely possess equal ability in batting and base-running. Therefore, it is the coach's duty to analyze the capabilities of his players and distribute their respective strengths in the batting order. In general, a well-balanced batting order places the team's strongest hitters at the top of the batting list, to assure them a maximum number of times at bat. Assuming the players are available, a well-balanced batting order would follow a generally prescribed pattern.

The first batter should be one with a special talent for getting on base. He should have a keen batting eye and not be tempted to swing at bad pitches. He should be fast of foot and a good base runner. Seldom will he swing at first pitches when no one is on base, since normally he will not be a power hitter. He may be an effective bunter, and if so, he will keep the defense on edge, since they will not know what he is going to do. His speed will often cause the defense to hurry their play on him, causing errors.

The number-two batter should be a skillful bunter and an excellent hit-and-run man. He need not be a long ball hitter, but should be able to get the bat on the ball. Ideally, he is a left-handed choke hitter who has good control of the bat. A left-handed hitter in this spot will make it easier for the runner to steal. Speed is desirable to keep down double plays, but is not as necessary as it is for the first batter.

The number-three batter usually will be the player with the highest batting average on the team. He should be fast on his feet since he will have more opportunitites to score on hits by the fourth hitter. If the number-three man bats left-handed, the number four man should hit right-handed.

The fourth batter should be a long ball hitter who can hit with runners on base. The assumption is that one or two of the first three batters will reach base, and in this spot he will have the opportunity to drive in runs. The number-four batter may be one of the two best hitters on the team.

The fifth batter's qualifications are much the same as those of number four. If a consistent hitter is not available, stress should be placed on the ability to hit the long ball.

The sixth batter should have the same qualifications as the first batter with the added ability to drive in runs. He will have many opportunities because of the hitting abilities of the third, fourth and fifth batters. A real "clutch" hitter is an ideal player for this position.

The seventh batter has much the same qualifications as the second with more stress placed on hitting the long ball. Also the seventh batter could be a slower runner than the second hitter.

In professional ball where games are played every day, the catcher and the pitcher usually are placed in the eighth and ninth positions in the batting order. The reason for this is that pitchers will not play every day, and catchers may catch only certain pitchers, thus not playing daily. By hitting them in the eighth and ninth places in the order, they do not disrupt the daily line-up.

In amateur ball where the teams do not play daily, as in high school and college, the pitcher and the catcher may be placed in the batting order according to their hitting ability. Another factor in deciding if the pitcher hits ninth would be if he stays in the game or plays some other position after being removed from the mound. If he is no longer in the line-up, who will replace him in the batting order? This must be considered in making out the line-up in order to have an effective batting order.

The Defensive Line-Up. From the defensive standpoint, the strength of a team first is considered down the middle. This would include the pitcher, catcher, shortstop, second baseman and center-fielder. Then the first baseman, third baseman, left-fielder and right-fielder are chosen.

Many baseball experts say that pitching is as much as 75 per cent of the defensive strength of a team. If this be true, pitching must be given first consideration. In judging a pitcher, the coach must consider control as the most important asset in amateur baseball. A player with a good fast ball, mental poise, physical strength and endurance has all the basic tools for becoming an outstanding pitcher. But in amateur baseball these qualifications are rare. Size is not a factor in viewing prospects, but a player who has a loose throwing motion and can get the ball over the plate has a great chance of being a successful pitcher.

The catcher is second in importance since he is the field general. He should be someone who knows baseball, has good hands, and can handle all types of thrown balls. A man who has a strong throwing arm, is alert to the game situations, and is an aggressive leader is the ideal type to work behind the plate. Good size and speed are assets but not essentials.

Defensively, the second baseman has more responsibility than any other infielder, and he must be the second best fielder of ground balls on the team. Speed, quickness, and mental alertness are essential to his play. A strong throwing arm is a desired asset since he will make many throws to first base from the second base area.

The shortstop should have a strong throwing arm and be the best all-round fielder of ground balls on the team. He should have excellent speed and the ability to cover a great deal of ground.

The center-fielder's requirements are excellent speed, a strong throwing arm, and the ability to cover a lot of ground. He should be adept at judging fly balls and charging ground balls hit in his area.

The first baseman should have quick hands and be able to handle all types of throws in his direction. He does not have to be exceptionally fast, and his throwing arm is not as important as those of the other infielder, but he should be able to field ground balls and shift his feet at first base.

The third baseman must have a good pair of hands with quick reflexes and an accurate, reasonably strong throwing arm. He must be able to field slow hit balls quickly and block hard-hit ground balls.

The right fielder should have a strong throwing arm and be a good judge of fly balls. Speed is desirable but is not as essential as in center field.

The left-fielder may have the weakest arm of the three outfielders, but speed and fielding ability are of great importance. The left-fielder will usually have many fielding opportunities in amateur baseball.

Practice Routine. One of the primary duties of a baseball coach is to keep his players busy every minute of a practice session, to impress upon them that they must work to improve themselves. Practice with half the team merely standing around cannot be tolerated. Practice that is organized, with everyone busy and some teaching taking place, is ideal.

The team should set a definite practice time when everyone will be on the field. This helps in the organizing of the practice time. If some players can come to the field earlier, they should be encouraged to do so, since provision can be made for them to work on weaknesses.

The first responsibility of the players when they arrive on the field is to get themselves loose, their legs as well as their arms. The major part of any work out centers in batting practice. It is here that a coach can get the most from his time if he is organized.

Batting Practice. It is important for each player to take as many swings as possible during this period of time. Players, pitchers, or coaches with good control should pitch batting practice when the hitters are working on timing. However, on the last round it is advisable for someone to throw three-quarter speed and curve balls with no attempt to fool the batter. This increases their chances of hitting the ball and develops confidence. As practice progresses toward the opening game, the hitter should see more curve balls each day.

Every team has a policy concerning the number of balls bunted or the number of swings taken, so that all players have the same amount of practice. Some teams favor a certain number of swings, even though the ball is fouled or missed. By this procedure, the hitter more likely will swing at good pitches and thus increase the number of rounds of batting practice.

When the batter takes his last swing on each round, he runs it out to first base. Early in pre-season workouts, he should run straight through the base, concentrating on getting out of the batter's box. As the season approaches, he should make his turn at first base. Then as the pitcher takes his stretch and the next batter is bunting, the former hitter is working on getting his lead and jump on the pitcher to steal second.

A popular drill in batting practice is to play "base hit" between the infielders and the outfielders. Each group is allowed ten swings, depending on the time remaining in batting practice, and the group with the most total hits is the winner. The coach can reward the winners with additional swings or make the losers do additional running. The pitchers are used to shag in the outfield.

For a fast moving batting practice, several baseballs are desirable so the pitcher need not wait for the balls to reach him. Two ball bags should be used, one filled with balls on the mound for the pitcher and one for a shager on the edge of the grass back of second base (Diag. 1-1). The shager is placed in this position to avoid the danger of his being hit by a batted ball. It also eliminates the problem of balls being thrown on the mound or infield. All players are instructed to return batted balls to the shager, and they should be thrown on the ground to him, not in the air. This is usually a good job for a pitcher, since it requires a great deal of bending. When the shager begins to fill up his bag with baseballs, he takes them to the mound between hitters, so batting practice pitchers will always have plenty of balls on hand. This system keeps batting practice moving and places the shager in a relatively safe place.

It is a general practice to hit ground balls to the infielders during batting practice. The fungo hitters who have this duty should stand near the batting cage, but out of danger of being hit by a batted ball (Diag. 1-1). The fungo hitters should refrain from hitting the ball until the batter has hit the pitch, or the ball has passed the plate. This prevents injuries to infielders. In pre-season work outs each infielder should receive at least a hundred ground balls each day. If the first baseman has a protective wire screen, the infielders can throw to first base. Batting practice is also an excellent time for the infielders to work on the double play.

While the infielders are receiving their ground balls and taking batting practice, someone should hit fly balls to the outfielders. A few of the outfielders may be taking batting practice, while the others are fielding fly balls. It usually is best for the outfielders to line up and then have balls hit to their left and right. After a few practice sessions, the outfielders should have balls hit over their heads and in front of them.

If a player is not receiving fungos during batting practice, he should assume a fielding position and play the ball off the bat as he

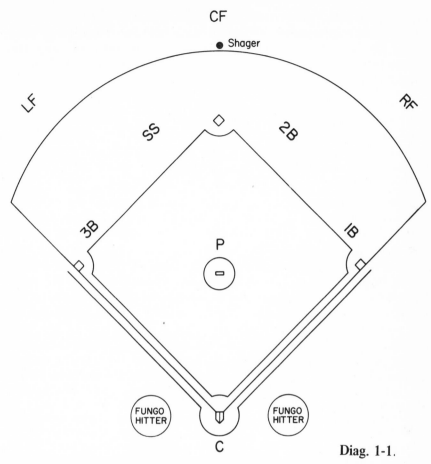

Diag. 1-1.

would in a game. One ball hit to a fielder off the bat in batting practice is worth ten balls hit off a fungo.

Game situations can be worked on during batting practice by placing runners on the bases and giving them certain directions. The runner then must react to where the ball is hit off the bat during batting practice. This works well with runners on second and third base concerning the decisions they must make in tagging up on fly balls and advancing on ground balls.

Many mechanical devices are available to facilitate batting practice, such as the batting tee, pitching machine, iso-swing, and protective screens for the pitcher.

The batting tee is beneficial in pre-season workouts if a player is having trouble with the angle of a swing in relation to the height of a pitch and the position of the ball over the place. A tee can help also to improve coordination of the stride and swing during a batting slump.

The pitching machine has merit, even though it does not simulate the action of a pitcher. In pre-season workouts the hitter needs to take as many swings as possible, and the machine can fill a need when no one who can get the ball over the plate is available. Lipscomb has a commercial-built machine placed inside an enclosed area where all hitters work on the straight, medium-speed pitches. After a round of thirty swings, the hitter moves to the diamond, where a pitcher is ready to throw curves and fastballs. This practice is beneficial to the pitcher as well as the hitter. By using the pitching machine, members of the team are able to take sixty swings almost every day and still have time for the other aspects of practice. The machine can be valuable in teaching the mechanics of bunting, wherein the bunting practice can be divorced from batting.

The iso-swing is excellent for hitters who have trouble rotating their hips into the swing. It can be placed on the side lines for them to work against. Hitters who have a lazy wrist swing and do not pull the ball will benefit from using the iso-swing.

A protective screen for the pitcher during batting practice is beneficial since he is less than sixty feet from the plate when the batter hits the ball. A screen about five feet high placed a proper distance in front of the pitching mound, so it does not worry the pitcher when he is throwing is advisable so that he can be fully protected after delivering the pitch.

Game Preparations. The coach should complete game plans several days in advance. The practice sessions should be tailored to fit the opposition. If the coach knows that the opponents will use a left-handed pitcher against him, his batting practice should be against left-handed throwing. If he thinks the opposing team may use a curve-ball pitcher, batting practice should be against someone throwing curves. Careful analysis and planning can win ball games before the players take the field.

It is sound procedure to discuss the known strength and weakness of the opposition with all team members present. Discuss the hitting abilities, the speed of the players, the throwing abilities of the outfielders, and any other points that may have a bearing on the game.

The coach should instruct the pitchers who may be used to take a thorough workout two days before the game. The day before the game they should throw very little, and the workout should be easy.

General practice the day before the game should be cut short, under normal conditions. Usually one hour and thirty minutes is ample time. But if the team has been losing or bad weather has limited the practice time, the coach may want to work out longer.

Pre-Game Batting Practice. In pre-game batting practice the infielders should receive several ground balls off a fungo bat, and the outfielders should play the balls from the bat. Then during infield practice, the outfielders will receive their fungos. If the team is playing on an unfamiliar field, this will give them an opportunity to adjust to the surroundings.

At the end of pre-game batting practice, most teams will bring the starters in to take some extra swings. They usually are allowed one swing each until the time runs out. During this period a little spirit and life should get into the squad. The players who are not starting should spread over the outfield to chase the balls.

All batting practice is intended primarily for the benefit of the hitter, especially pre-game hitting. But this does not indicate that slow pitches should be thrown to the batter. This type of batting practice does more harm than good. The batter needs to see some three-quarter speed pitches, along with curve balls. There should be no attempt to fool the batter. Some coaches like for the pitchers to throw full speed when the hitters are called in at the end of pre-game batting practice. Other coaches like for straight three-quarter speed pitches to be thrown, so the hitter can develop his confidence.

While batting practice is in progress, the coach should be on the field, reminding players of special instructions. He should call attention to the wind, the sun, and any peculiarities of the playing area. He should instruct the pitcher concerning the amount of time to warm up according to the weather conditions. The outfielders should be reminded of the effects of wind conditions on fly balls. The coach should verify all arrangements with outfield fungo hitters, relay men, and fungo fielders. Additional infielders who are to take part in the infield workout should be notified. Any other advice that will help win the game should be exploited by the coach. Batting practice can be boring or interesting, depending on what is done and the organization the coach has placed on this period of time. Baseball games are won or lost during practice sessions.

During the opposition's batting practice session, the coach and his entire squad should observe the hitters. Possible batting weaknesses that are detected should be discussed by coach, pitcher and catcher. The infielders and outfielders should be making mental notes on who pulls the ball or hits late.

Infielders and outfielders should warm up again for a few minutes before infield practice by throwing.

Outfield-Infield Routine. Fielding practice is an important part of baseball. It is important that a team get the most from this type of practice. For this to be done, each player must be warmed up adequately, so that he can throw hard without hurting his arm. Also, such a practice routine must be organized to present game-like situations.

Usually two or three ground balls are hit to each outfielder at the start of the practice, so that throws may be made to second and third base and to the plate. The infielders cover bases and take their various cut-off positions on such throws to practice the duties they are expected to perform in the game.

The coach generally hits to the outfield from a point near the pitcher's mound for throws by the outfielders, and he may hit infield practice from either side of the plate. Fungos to the outfielders are usually hit before infield practice, and during infield practice the outfielders take additional fly balls. These fungos are hit from a spot on the outfield side of the infield to avoid striking anyone.

The outfielders' routine of throwing to the various bases consists of three rounds of two throws each. The routine consists of the following:

Round 1
   1. LF to 2B (hit ball near left-field line)
   2. CF to 2B (hit ball to left of center field)
   3. RF to 2B (hit ball near right field line)
Round 2
   1. LF to 3B (hit ball to left-center field)
   2. CF to 3B (hit ball straight to center field)
   3. RF to 3B (hit ball straight to right field)
Round 3
   1. LF to C (hit ball to left field)
   2. CF to C (hit ball to center field)
   3. RF to C (hit ball to right field)

A common infield routine consists of approximately six rounds during which each infielder and the catcher field a ball to complete one round. The number may be increased to seven or eight rounds. Prior to the first round, a good procedure is to have the infield in, with the throw going to the plate, and the ball being hit at each infielder. This routine works on cutting the runner down at the plate. At the end of practice each infielder fields a slowly hit ball and throws to first base. On these two routines the catcher does not throw to the bases.

The following six rounds are standard procedures for infield practice, in which the ball is hit to the first player listed and then thrown around the infield as indicated by the bases or plate:

Round 1 (to first base; ball hit directly at each man)
   1. 3B-1B-C-3B-2B-1B-C
   2. SS-1B-C-SS-3B-C
   3. 2B-1B-C-2B-3B-C
   4. 1B-SS-1B-C
   5. C-1B-SS-C

Round 2

Same as first round except hit the ball to infielder's left.

Round 3 (double play: ball hit infielder's left)

1. 3B-2B-1B-C-3B-C
2. SS-2B-1B-C-SS-C
3. 2B-SS-1B-C-2B-C
4. 1B-SS-1B-C
5. C-SS-1B-C

Round 4

Same as third round except hit the ball to infielder's right.

Round 5 (to first base: ball hit to infielder's right)

Same as Round 1 and 2

Round 6

The ball is hit slowly to each infielder, and the throw is made to first base as he charges in. The infielder continues off the field to complete infield practice.

In order to complete the above fielding routine in ten minutes, which is usually allotted for pre-game infield and outfield practice, the coach uses at least three baseballs. This allows for balls getting by the defense. The coach should try to keep two balls in play, hitting a second ball just as the ball previously hit completes a cycle.

Charts, Records, and Notes. A coach, unless he has an exceptional memory, can help himself very much by keeping charts, records and notes on his own personnel and the opposition. Some of the observations will have to be made and recorded during a game or practice sessions. Other observations are recorded after the day's work or before practice the next day. Over a period of years, the author has learned it is better "not to put to memory what can be written down."

Some system of recording a pitcher's performance, pitch by pitch, throughout the game can be very useful to both the pitcher and the coach. A very simple method of recording each pitch inside or outside of the strike zone and what pitches were thrown is shown on a stenciled card for each opposing batter (Diag. 1-2).

The following numbers are used to indicate the type of pitch delivered: a fast ball is 1; a breaking pitch is 2; and a change of pace is 3. By using symbols along with the numbers, every move of a hitter can be charted. For example, if the batter gets a base hit to centerfield, the chart will show 1H8. The batter hit a fast ball, 1; for a base hit, H; and to centerfield, 8. The following are other examples of how the symbols work:

2F9 - breaking ball flied to right field.

1K - strike out on fast ball.

1P4 - fast ball popped to second base.
3L7 - change of pace lined to left field.
1H9 - a fast ball hit for base hit to right field.
1E5 - fast ball hit to third base who error the ball.

First Batter _____
Bats   _____

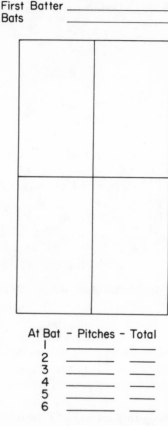

At Bat - Pitches - Total
 1   _____   ____
 2   _____   ____
 3   _____   ____
 4   _____   ____
 5   _____   ____
 6   _____   ____   **Diag. 1-2.**

    The card lists the player's number, his name, and whether he bats right or left. It also has a place for comments, which may list if he is fast or slow and his type of batting stance. These types of notes are very helpful if the opposition is to be played again.

    As each pitch is made, its location with relation to the strike zone and what happened is recorded. The number of pitches is recorded at the bottom of the card for each turn at bat, and a running total is kept for the number of pitches thrown in the game. The pitcher may weaken and lose control in a late inning, and the coach may want to analyze the number of pitches thrown in the game, particularly the last few innings. The average nine inning game should require no more than 125 pitches. If a pitcher is relieved, a notation is made, and the number of pitches he throws is recorded.

The chart that has been discussed is attempting to show the following:

1. What pitches were called balls and strikes;
2. The quality of the pitcher's control;
3. What pitches were hit well or poorly;
4. The total number of pitches thrown;
5. What type of pitches were used;
6. Characteristics of the hitters.

In keeping this type of chart, two individuals should work together and discuss with the battery what the opposing batters did the last time up. If there are any weaknesses or strong points, the pitcher and catcher should be aware of this before they face the batter the next time.

Some coaches like to chart their own hitters, hoping to detect any batting faults. If the batter is conscious that every pitch is being recorded, he may be more aware of his strike zone. An idea here that the author has used is to get someone in the community, maybe an ex-professional baseball player, to chart the hitters and make notes concerning his observations. Many times someone like this will spot something the coach is overlooking.

During the game or in practice the coach should have a clip-board handy to record observations he makes concerning what is happening on the field. These notes should be thoroughly analyzed before they are discussed with the players. Such observations can be the difference between winning or losing. How many times has a coach thought of something he should cover in practice and then forgotten it, only to have this omission cost him a game a few weeks later! Sometimes seemingly minor notations prove to be very important. Notes will not necessarily win ball games, but they do help the coach work toward better organization, and they are of great value in answering questions that may arise in his mind.

The author has found that notes taken during the off-season are very helpful the next spring. Thoughts that occur during reading or discussing baseball with other coaches are better written down than left to memory for the next season.

2

EARLY SEASON TRAINING
AND CONDITIONING

For a baseball player to be effective and to perform consistently, he must be in excellent physical condition. One job of the coach is to get the players into top physical condition before the season starts and to keep them that way throughout the entire schedule. A player should start his conditioning program about a month before regular practice sessions begin. This pre-practice work should consist of throwing, running, stretching and weight-training.

This type of physical conditioning requires self-discipline. If a player who has ability does not believe in the necessity of conditioning, ultimately he will let the team down. The outstanding player wants to be in superior physical shape so he can perform at his full potential at all times. Genuine self-discipline involves not only conditioning but other daily activities such as studying, eating, and sleeping.

Pre-Season Conditioning. Running is hard work, but it is the most beneficial exercise known to man. Early pre-season conditioning should include a great deal of running. Strong legs and stamina are important to a ball player. All players should run, but this is doubly true of pitchers. During the first week running should be in the form of laps, with the individual doing some type of slow running. After the first week, it should change to the form of wind-sprints.

Stretching exercises which will prevent pulled muscles in legs, back, and arms are very important, also, to all baseball players, especially the pitchers. Before a player ever throws a baseball, he should do some stretching exercises.

Stretching the arms is a very simple procedure which a player can do by hanging from a bar or any other object above his head. All players should stretch at least one minute per day on a bar, and pitchers should use the hanging exercise at least two minutes each day. After repeating this daily for two weeks, the players can begin hanging by the throwing arm only.

Other stretching exercises which the player should do every day he takes the field are trunk rotation, bending to the side, bend and reach, and stretching the groin. They will help not only in conditioning, but in many cases will prevent muscle damage.

After a player has completed his stretching, he can begin to throw easily. Each player should throw every day, but not hard until his arm is in shape and properly warmed up. At Lipscomb the number of sore arms has been reduced considerably since the team started throwing without a glove the first three weeks in January. The author has found this method to be successful in keeping the players from throwing too hard too soon.

Weight-training is not designed to develop large muscles for the baseball player, but to build muscle tone and strength. To increase strength, the part being developed must be overloaded. To overload is to force the part to a maximum effort to overcome a resistance. When more resistance is added, more muscle fibers must be brought into play to overcome the resistance—thus the growth is strength. It is important in any strength-building program continuously to increase the amount of resistance.

For many years the use of weights for baseball players was frowned upon. Most baseball experts feared that the player would become muscle-bound and lose the whiplike action that is needed. In the past few years, authorities have changed their views, since several professional players owe a great part of their success to weight-lifting programs.

A weight-lifting program must be well-planned and carefully supervised. A player must understand the specific purpose for each exercise. He must know that some types of lifting can be harmful to him as a baseball player and that none is being done to add bulk but to increase strength and speed.

Calisthenics lack the efficiency of weights to develop strength, since too much time is required to overload a muscle group. But such calisthenics as jumping-jack, trunk twister, knee bends, sit-ups and leg raises do play an important role in maintaining body flexibility.

The use of isometric exercises in conditioning has received considerable attention in the field of athletics. In executing an isometric exercise, the part of the body being developed pushes or pulls against an object or another part of the body. These types of exercises consume very little time and are becoming very popular with a great many coaches. Their weaknesses is their inability to build endurance and flexibility.

In-Season Conditioning. Perhaps the most neglected phase of baseball training is in-season conditioning. Coaches spend a great deal of time developing strength, flexibility, and stamina in pre-season workout, but do very little, if anything, in-season to maintain the same level. Once the season begins, running is the only exercise continued. This is good for the legs and the cardio-vascular system, but it does not maintain strength and flexibility.

A study done at Lipscomb by the author and Dr. Glen Reeder of George Peabody College showed that throughout the season the baseball players tested did not maintain the level of strength with which they started. Of twenty baseball players checked at the beginning, mid-point, and end of the season, only one individual maintained the same level of strength. The season consisted of 32 games.

The author believes that baseball coaches need to revise their in-season conditioning program with a realistic view toward what is taking place in practice. Playing the game and running in practice will neither develop nor maintain strength throughout the season. The author does not recommend a weight-lifting program in season, but such exercises as push-ups, pull-ups, squeezing a rubber ball and the wrist rollup, which will be explained in the conditioning drills, are helpful for maintaining strength in the arms, wrists, and shoulders.

A coach should never let a baseball player get out of physical condition during the season. The principle of continuous conditioning is one that should apply to baseball teams. Some people believe that baseball players are poorly conditioned athletes, and perhaps in a few cases they are right. But those individuals who make the best contribution to the team over the entire season are the players who train continually and keep their bodies in top physical condition.

Conditioning for Pitchers. Physical conditioning in the early season for pitchers must not be overlooked. A pitcher may have outstanding ability, but if he lacks stamina, he may be of little value to the team. He will tire in the late innings of games and will hurt the team in the latter part of the season. If his legs are shaky and his arm is tired, he is not in full command of the situation.

The schedule of conditioning in the pre-season should be varied according to the length of the early season, the age, and the physical condition of the pitcher. In a situation where there are only a few weeks of early season practice before the first game, the schedule will have to be accelerated. If the practice starts in January or February, the schedule can be extended. Some teams start the pitchers throwing indoors in January. If this is done, their arms should be in excellent shape by the time the first game is played.

The pitcher who reports for the first practice in good condition should be able to pitch several innings within a few weeks. In the beginning the coach lets each pitcher throw a certain number of pitches, increasing the number each day. At Lipscomb after four weeks of throwing, in January, the pitchers begin to pitch an inning every other day. An inning consists of twenty pitches, which are thrown to a catcher who is giving signals and mixing the pitches. The pitcher should be throwing about 80% of his total effort; since it is early, there is no reason to throw 100%. After the pitcher has thrown one inning, he sits down while another member of the staff throws one inning. They continue rotating until the prescribed number of innings have been pitched. They do this every other day, because they should never throw hard two consecutive days.

During this early period of training, the development of endurance, the learning of new skills, and the improvement of old ones should be stressed. Running, throwing, and exercises for agility are important. When the pitcher does his throwing, control should be stressed. During the first few weeks it may be erratic, but with practice and concentration steady improvement should be seen.

After the season starts, the coach should know the capabilities of the pitcher and what he needs to stress each day. From this point forward, the emphasis should be on improvement in skills and on maintaining good physical conditioning.

As a general rule, pitchers do very little throwing and no running the day before they are scheduled to pitch. Any throwing should be for control. The amount done earlier in the week will depend on the way the pitcher's arm feels. The coach should work out a routine to fit the needs of each individual pitcher. The main objective is to maintain conditioning and to improve his skills.

On baseball teams which have only one or two pitchers, the routine for pitching can be a problem. It is usually not recommended on the high school level or below to start a pitcher twice a week. If there is a shortage, the coach may start him one game and use him in relief in the next. If a pitcher starts on Monday and throws a large number of pitches, he should rest on Tuesday, loosen up on Wednesday, and be ready for relief on Thursday.

If the squad is so small that there are not enough pitchers to throw batting practice, the coach should use infielders and outfielders who can get the ball over the plate. The amount of throwing done by the infielders and outfielders during batting practice will depend on the fielder's throwing arm.

Problems with Staleness. All coaches have experienced the problem of staleness, when a player in top condition suddenly gives a performance below his proven ability. He may be tired and lack enthusiasm when on the field. This situation may last for several days or longer, depending on the cause.

Generally the factors producing staleness are excessive fatigue, worry, and change of attitude. Any of these problems may cause a loss of appetite and usually a loss of weight.

Overwork or monotony of the routine may result in excessive fatigue, which will show on the field in a lack of enthusiasm and zest for play. Overwork may be caused by the individual having to do physical work besides baseball or by heavy mental work in school by a college player. To eliminate excessive fatigue, the coach should consider reducing the overall practice time and giving the squad a day off when the schedule permits it.

Worry is another problem with which coaches must contend. The player may be upset over studies, finances, romance or conditions at home. It is best if the coach can get the player to discuss these problems with him. They are not easily solved, but a sympathetic listener generally helps.

The coach is usually able to detect a change in attitude toward practice and the game. The player shows discouragement and sometimes disgust with what is taking place on the field. The coach should have a conference with him discussing any problems he may have, and giving him encouragement by stressing his strong points.

Conditioning Drills. *Pick-Ups:* This is one of the most effective conditioning drills for coordination, agility, and endurance. It is done by having one player in a stationary position about ten feet away roll a ball to another player from one side to another in an arc of about twelve feet. The receiver must pick up the ball with two hands and return it with an underhand toss. This exercise should be started with about twenty-five pick-ups and increased until one hundred is reached on a once-a-day basis in pre-season conditioning. In addition to running, it should be continued all season by the pitchers.

Wrist Roll-Up: The coach can make a roll-up by drilling a hole through a handle and placing a rope through the hole. The other end of the rope will have a ten to twenty-pound weight on it. The player can execute the wrist roll-up by keeping his palms down, arms high, elbows straight, and slowly rolling the weight up to the rope. (Fig. 2-1). The exercise should be repeated up and down slowly three to five times each day.

Football Pass Drill: The coach assumes a position near the edge of the infield, behind second base. The squad takes a starting position on the right field foul line, each player with a baseball in his hand. At a starting signal, a player runs past the coach and tosses him the ball as he passes. The player continues to run towards the left field foul line until the coach calls his name, then he cuts towards the outfield to receive the thrown baseball from the coach. When each player has had his turn, all line up on the left field foul line and run past the

Fig. 2-1.

coach, again, giving him the baseball and receiving another throw along the right field line.

Stretching Drill: Players pair off to work this drill. Player A should be in bent knee stance with arms and hands ready to catch the ball. Player B should toss the ball just out of reach of Player A, making him lean or reach for it. In trying to catch the ball, Player A must not move his feet but may use his non-catching hand for support in reaching for it. After one player has caught a prescribed number of tosses, they change positions.

Twenty-five Drill: This is an excellent team or individual conditioning drill with which to end a day's practice. A series of activities should be performed as follows:

(a) Jog 50 yards and walk back to starting point. Repeat five times.

(b) At starting point do five push ups.

(c) Sprint 50 yards and walk back to starting point. Repeat five times.

(d) At starting point do five push-ups.

The above routine is followed until each player has run twenty-five sprints and has done twenty-five push-ups. The coach may increase the number of repetitions as the season advances.

Bench Drill: The players stand in front of a bench about eighteen inches high. Each player alternates placing his feet on the bench in rhythmic movements of the legs and arms. This can be done daily during pre-season training but should be discontinued during regular season play. It is an outstanding drill to develop the legs. The number of step-ups will depend on the age group and the other training devices used by the coach.

Base Running Drill: The coach uses this drill to increase the speed of the base runners by using a stop watch to time each member of the squad as he circles the bases. It is done outside and after the players' legs are in shape. The watch should be started with the crack of the bat, and college players should complete the circuit in seventeen seconds. Each player's time should be recorded and results placed on the bulletin board in the locker room to stimulate competition. This is an ideal time to stress proper base running techniques, to cut down on the time.

Reaction Drill: In this drill the squad should be arranged in pairs. Player A spreads his legs and bends his body at the waist. Player B stands about three feet from Player A with a baseball, which he attempts to toss, roll, or bounce between Player A's legs without his catching it. Player A is not allowed to use a glove or move his feet, but B can fake him in any direction as long as he does not move his feet. This drill requires stretching on the part of Player A and will develop his reflexes. After a period of time, the two rotate positions. The coach can make the drill competitive.

Mile Run: This drill can be done as a group or individually. Each player holds a standing position taking 100 running steps in place before stopping. Then he does 15 side-straddle hops· with hands clapping over head. This sequence is repeated five times in early season and can be increased as conditioning improves.

Fungo Drill: The players line up on the right field foul line, and each takes his turn, running hard to center field, where the coach hits a fly ball to be caught on the run. It is caught or retrieved and returned to the vicinity of the mound, where the coach is using a fungo bat to hit the fly balls. After the player returns the ball to the mound, he continues jogging to the left field foul line. Once over and back constitutes a trip, and the coach can increase the number of trips each day. This drill is excellent to develop endurance.

Pitcher Conditioner: After the pitcher has completed his throwing for the day, he goes to the outfield with the coach and faces him about 30 yards away. The coach has several baseballs and an assistant, who is a pitcher waiting his turn. The coach throws a series of fly balls in various directions for the pitcher to catch in the air and throw to the assistant. As soon as a ball is caught or missed, the coach throws another in the opposite direction. The pitcher must catch 25 without a miss. If a ball is missed, one is counted off the number already successfully caught. The number of catches can be increased daily. The pitcher should shower immediately following this drill.

Pepper Game: The pepper game can be beneficial in conditioning for the fielders and batters. It provides practice for the batter in keeping his eyes on the ball and in place hitting. The drill gives the fielder practice in fielding and should sharpen his reflexes. It should never involve more than four fielders and one hitter in any one group.

The fielders should line up about 25 feet from the batter and a few yards apart, so that they will have room to make plays to either side. Each batter should hit 25 or 30 balls, and then the fielder who is head of the line becomes the batter. The original batter goes to the foot of the line, and the players continue rotating until each fielder has become the hitter.

Indoor Drills. A major problem which confronts most baseball coaches is getting a team ready to play when the weather conditions prevent the players from going outdoors on a regular basis. The following are "foul" weather drills which can be used in a gymnasium.

Check Pitching Action: Place a strip of tape on the gymnasium floor, representing a pitcher's rubber. Stick a 2 inch strip of tape perpendicular to the rubber at the point where the pivot foot (right for right-handers, left for left-handers) rests on the rubber (Fig. 2-2). The pitcher should throw to a catcher, and the coach should watch where the pitcher's feet land. If the left foot of a right-hander is not landing to the left of the tape, he is throwing across his body, which means he is losing speed and control.

Fig. 2-2.

Hit the Knee: Pitchers stretch and throw to the first baseman who is in a position of holding the runner tight with his right foot nearest the base. The pitcher continues throwing until he is able to throw accurately to the first baseman's right knee.

Pitcher Recovery: The pitcher takes his wind-up and throws the ball to the catcher. The coach immediately throws a tennis ball to the pitcher, thereby requiring him to return quickly to a ready position. Pitchers are instructed to pitch, gain balance, raise the glove, and field their position. The tennis ball simulates a line-drive through the pitcher's box.

Covering First Base: Line up the pitchers near the middle of the gymnasium, place the first baseman in his position, and place a base in its proper relation to the pitcher and the fielder. Throw ground ball to the first baseman, with the pitcher taking the correct path to the base to receive the toss. Stress catching the ball a couple of steps before reaching the base, so that he can look down as he tags the base.

Pitching to String Target: Construct a strike zone by using strings of some type of cord which will not break easily. The upper string should be at armpit level and the lower at knee level. Two vertical strings are tied the width of home plate, which is 17 inches. Volleyball standards in the gym may be used for the string attachments. The pitcher should throw to the catcher, who is in full gear behind the target. As the pitchers sharpen their control, extra strings may be added to help them work on spot pitching.

Follow-Through Drill: The pitcher loosens up his arm and becomes ready to throw hard. When he begins throwing hard, he must bend over and touch the gym floor on his follow through. He should repeat this until bending his back becomes a habit. Pitchers continually throwing high usually are in an upright position. If this drill is practiced outside, the pitcher may pick up a stone or stick and then replace it for the next pitch.

Mass Lead-Off: Have five runners take their leads off a base at the end of the gym floor. Let the pitcher assume his position in proper relation to first base. As he stretches, the runners lead off towards the other end of the floor. The pitcher may go through his delivery with a medium speed throw to the catcher or a pick-off throw to first base, which should not be thrown hard. If the delivery is made to the plate, the runners sprint to the other end of the floor, and a new group of runners take their place. The pitchers are practicing holding the runner on the base, and the runners have worked on getting the good fast break towards second without being picked off.

Medicine Ball: Place a heavy medicine ball on a small table or stand and let the batter swing through it, trying to knock it off the table. He should be instructed to break his wrists and roll his hips as he makes contact. This exercise develops techniques which are important to good hitting.

Bunt the Ball: Lightweight mats which aid in slowing the roll of the bunted ball are placed on the floor in the entire bunting area. This drill is live with a pitcher throwing medium speed to the batter, who squares around and bunts the ball. A backstop can be constructed by raising the parallel bars to their maximum height and placing a lightweight mat over them.

Batting Practice: The coach can take batting practice in the gymnasium by using tennis balls or a soft rubber covered ball made by Dudley Sports Company. The coach or any player except a pitcher can throw the tennis balls or rubber balls at three-quarter speed. Each player swings away as in regular batting practice. This is the next best thing to hitting outside unless the team has a machine set up in the gym.

Run-Down: Put down two bases 90 feet apart, and divide the infielders, stationing one-half behind each base designated as first and second. Outfielders who will not participate in the run-down may be the trapped base runners. The coach should give instruction as to the run-down method he wishes to employ before this drill is started.

Sliding Drill: Players should report in sliding pads and sweat suits. An area approximately 6 feet by 5 feet should be marked out with sweeping compound and a small canvas or blanket placed over it. Put a base on top of the blanket, and have the players slide into it. Since the floor is slick and the blanket will slide, it approximates outdoor conditions.

Double Play: This drill is for the second baseman and the shortstop to work together on the double play on half of the gymnasium floor. They can work on throwing properly to the bases and making the pivot. If the coach has room, he may allow the throw to be made to first base after the pivot. The coach may roll a ball to the shortstop, who throws to second, and the second baseman makes the pivot. If there is a first baseman, he can throw to him. Be sure the infielders concentrate on footwork and the proper throw.

Catcher's Drill: Dress the catchers in full equipment, place them against a wall, and make wild throws to them. They should be in their natural catching position and be instructed on how to shift their feet to stay in front of the ball. As the coach makes throws, they should stop low pitches and position themselves to allow the ball to bounce off their chests towards the playing field. The catcher should resume his normal position after each pitch.

Catcher Foot Placement: Catchers in full gear assume their normal catching position. The ball is thrown so they are required to execute proper footwork for high, low, outside, pitchout, and intentional walk.

Relay Man: Each thrower holds a ball, with his back turned to the relay men. On a given signal all throwers turn and throw to the relay man opposite their position. Throwers attempt to throw the ball at shoulder high level in order to assure ease of handling and rapid relay. Relay men extend their arms, providing a good target for the throw.

Secure the Ball: An outfielder sprints straight ahead and catches a ball thrown by the coach. He takes a low throw, tumbles to the mat, then throws to the catcher. Players are instructed to squeeze the ball, execute a shoulder roll, and recover quickly for a speedy and accurate throw. The occasional use of a tennis ball emphasizes the need for squeezing the ball.

Throw to Third: The catcher receives the pitched ball and throws to third base under the pressure of the right-handed batter. The third baseman returns the ball to the pitcher, who pitches to the next catcher.

Ignore the Runner: Ground balls are hit to the infielders at varying speeds. Runners run in front of the infielder at different distances, attempting to distract him.

Outfielders Drill: The ball is thrown right, left, short or long, and the outfielders move quickly to recover the ball, executing proper footwork. The drill can be used outdoors also.

First Baseman Drill: Place a base against the gym wall and have the first baseman put his heels against the outside edge of the base. The coach or a player can toss or make throws to the first baseman while he practices on proper footwork.

Diamond Drills. *Multiple Situation Drills:* This is a very effective drill to show all the situations that may occur in a game. The coach will place his basic line-up at each position. The remaining pitchers and substitutes will form a single line behind home plate, since they are designated as base runners. The coach stands in the batter's box with a fungo bat and ball. As the catcher receives the ball from the pitcher, the coach makes a play by hitting the ball in his possession. The first player in the line runs to first when the ball is hit and reacts to situations as though he were in a game. If he is successful, he becomes the base runner.

As this drill is practiced, many game situations will develop to present the infield and outfield with ample opportunities to practice their play-making ability, while the pitcher can practice holding men on base. The coach can set up special situations any time during this drill to see how the team will react.

Pitcher and Infield Drill: Here two drills are incorporated into one. The pitchers are working on covering first base on ground balls to the first and second basemen. At the same time the shortstop and third basemen are fielding ground balls and throwing to second base. The coach will need his complete infield and all his pitchers. The outfielders serve as base runners. The coach must coordinate his fungo hitters to hit at the same time.

The pitcher holds the runner close at first base and then throws to the catcher. As the ball passes over the plate, both fungoes are hit. The pitcher covers first or fields the ball and throws to first. The third basement and shortstop field their ground ball and make a play at second base on the runner advancing from first. The runner from home plate stays at first, and the runner on second stays for the next pitch and scores on it.

Rapid-Fire Drill: This drill is used to help infielders orient themselves to bases so that they can throw quickly and accurately without wasting time. The infielder is placed in his position, with the first baseman covering first. The coach or player hits eight balls in rapid-fire order to the infielder, who throws to first. Each ball is hit before the infielder has time to get set. The drill is continued until all infielders have fielded at least 15 balls. It can be varied with throws to different bases and the plate.

Squeeze Play: Line up all the players at third base except the pitcher, the catcher and a batter. The first player in the line is the base runner at third base. He takes his normal advance during the windup and breaks for the plate as the pitcher is about to release the ball. The batter must bunt the ball on the ground regardless of where the pitch is made. The pitcher should be trying to throw the ball close to the strike zone. The coach should watch the runners very closely to see that they leave for home plate at the proper time. The base runner becomes the batter, and the former batter goes to the end of the line at third base.

Multiple Infield Practice: The coach places all the infielders in their positons, including the utility infielders. Each fielding position has a fungo hitter, who hits to that position only. If there are extra fielders, they take turns. The infielders throw the ball directly back to the fungo hitter, who may have someone shagging for him.

This drill may be planned so the infielders will throw to certain bases. For example, the extra second baseman could take throws from third base or shortstop while the regular second baseman fields all ground balls.

This drill gives each infielder a maximum number of ground balls in a short period of time.

Alternate Double Play: This drill provides work on the alternate double play when the second to first play can not be made. The coach puts runners on first and third with the infield in double play depth, the pitcher on the mound, and the catcher behind the plate. A ball is hit sharply to an infielder or the pitcher. The player fielding the ball "looks" the runner back to third and throws to second for one out. The runner on third breaks for home when the throw is made to second base. The fielder who covers second base throws to the catcher at the plate. The catcher makes the tag on the runner for the second out of the double play.

Playing the Sun: Place outfielders in a position so that all fungo balls will be directly in the sun, which should be behind the hitter's back. Fungos hit by the coach will simulate actual hitting in a game situation. This is an excellent way to teach outfielders to play the sun with or without sun glasses. If the outfielder does use sun glasses, he must know exactly where the ball is, before he flips his glasses down to make the catch. Flipping the glasses too early will cause the outfielder to lose the ball or misjudge it. Playing the sun and using sun glasses require a great deal of practice.

Hitting the Relay Man: Place all outfielders and infielders in their proper places. The coach should hit to all positions in the outfield, and have the outfielders make all plays which they must throw to the relay man. The relay man should have his arms in the air when the outfielder makes a quick hard overhand throw to him, which should be head high and on the glove side.

The Flincher: The coach places all the infielders in their proper positions but on the edge of infield grass. He will hit sharp ground balls to the infielders, who throw to the plate to keep a runner from scoring. The throw is very important, since it should be low, so the catcher can tag the sliding runner. The runner will be simulated, but the throw should be accurate. The coach may hit slow ground balls, also, and the infielders may go to first base with the ball.

Bunt Defense Drill: The purpose of this drill is to develop teamwork and practice defensing the bunt. The team takes its positions on the field while substitutes act as bunters and runners. Pitchers work from the stretch and throw strikes so the batter can bunt. The infielders and outfielders carry out their assignments. Every bunt situation should be covered in this drill. The pitchers and regulars should be changed, so that everyone will have a chance to participate. The coach should stress the duty of the catcher to call out the play.

Pitcher Throwing to Second: The purpose of this drill is to practice the timing on the throw from the pitcher to second base after he has fielded a batted ball. The pitcher, first baseman, shortstop, and third baseman are used in this drill. The coach hits a ball back to the pitcher, who pivots and throws to second base. The shortstop and the second baseman should rotate in receiving the throws. The pitcher should be told who will cover the base before the ball is hit. Following completion of the throw, either infielder covering at second base should throw to first base for the double play. Because of the timing element and the angle of the throw, this play requires a great deal of practice.

Part II

OFFENSIVE BASEBALL

3

HITTING FOR THE AVERAGE

Though, fundamentally, hitting is a natural skill, it can be improved with intelligent analysis and diligent practice.

No two players hit in exactly the same way, and the boy who hits well naturally should be left alone. Only when the coach decides that a correction can improve the batter should a change be suggested.

The superior hitter is always observing the situation. While sitting on the bench, he watches the pitcher. He looks for tip-offs, the actual pitching move, the pitching pattern, and particularly, the hurler's most effective pitch. The catcher will call for this pitch more frequently against the good hitters and when a hit will mean a run. Although the outstanding hitter will not do much guessing, he can often anticipate the pitch by intelligent observation.

The batter carries two types of equipment with him to the plate—mental and physical. The quality of these properties and their coordination will determine the kind of hitter he will be.

Physical Aspect. *Selection of the Bat:* The player should choose a bat that feels right to him and one that he can control. If the bat is not balanced, it will swing him rather than his swinging the bat.

Many power-conscious players use a bat that is too heavy or too long for them. The result is a loss of control and balance, with a consequent impairment in the all-important factor of timing.

The recommended length bat for the average hitter is 33 or 34 inches, with 34 preferred for the college hitter. Since most major league players favor this length, it stands to reason that the younger and less mature hitter should use a shorter and lighter bat, rather than a longer and heavier one.

The fact that most pitchers are fastballers places even greater emphasis on a light bat. As the season lengthens and muscles grow tired, even many big leaguers will switch to a lighter bat.

The weight of the bat should be a few ounces less than its length. The wood should be straight and narrow-grained, as this type provides a harder surface that furnishes more driving power.

A player can do several things to keep his bat in good condition. If possible, he should not permit other players to use it. He should rub it down with a dry bone or a bottle to keep it from chipping, and he should be sure not to throw it around carelessly. It is essential to keep a bat as dry as possible. Whenever it gets wet, a light coating of oil should be rubbed into it. Another precaution is for the batter to turn the trademark down in batting practice so the same side will not be taking all the contact.

Gripping the Bat: Good hitting is nearly impossible without a comfortable grip which permits an explosive swing. There are three types of grips.

The *end grip,* used mainly by power hitters, places the bottom hand close to or touching the knob of the bat (Fig. 3-1).

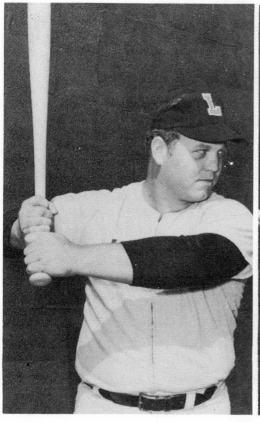 

Fig. 3-1.   Fig. 3-2.

The *modified grip* furnishes better bat control and still produces power. As shown in the photo, the hands are placed a few inches above the knob (Fig. 3-2).

The *choke grip* is used by non-power hitters who want to place or "punch" the ball sharply. As shown, the hands are placed well above the knob (Fig. 3-3).

Fig. 3-3.

Any grip must give the hands and wrists complete freedom of movement. The bat should be gripped primarily in the fingers, not back in the palms, with the knuckles of the top hand aligned

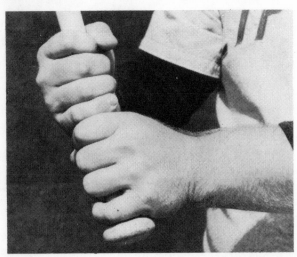

Fig. 3-4.

with the knuckles of the bottom hand (Fig. 3-4). This placement provides a more comfortable feel, allows a quicker reaction to the pitch, and produces the easy wrist action that supplies power.

Many hitters grip the bat too tightly prior to the swing. It should never be held so tightly as to whiten the knuckles. A tight grip will tense the forearm muscles and impair the swing.

The *stance* should be comfortable, placing the batter close enough to the plate to reach any ball in the strike zone.

To determine the proper location, the inexperienced hitter may move around until he can, by bending over slightly, just touch the outside edge of the plate with his bat (Fig. 3-5). This will assure full

Fig. 3-5.

plate coverage on a normal swing. With experience, the batter will be able to take his stance without going through the procedure.

The foot spread varies from batter to batter. Many players keep their feet too close together, forcing them to lunge at the ball. This tendency can be corrected by their taking a wider initial stance. Since the stride can be only so long, a wider spread will naturally shorten the stride and help to eliminate premature striding.

Most coaches think that the spread usually should be wider than the shoulders, with the stride no longer than eight to 10 inches. Many power hitters, however, take a longer stride.

The relationship of the feet to the plate is also important. There are three standard positionings: parallel, closed, and open.

In the *parallel stance,* both feet are approximately the same distance from the plate.

In the *closed stance,* the front foot is closer to the plate than the rear foot.

In the *open stance,* the front foot is farther from the plate than the rear foot.

Experimentation with these positionings may help the batter who is having trouble with specific kinds of pitches. For instance, if a player is having difficulty with the outside pitch, he may move closer to the plate and use a parallel stance. Some coaches contend that the open stance will help the batter against pitchers throwing from the same side (right vs. right, left vs. left).

Depth in the box must also be considered. Against pitchers who throw sinking fastballs and breaking pitches, a position toward the front of the box is preferred. If the hitter is standing deep in the box, he may not be able to reach the curve breaking over the outside part of the plate (Diag. 3-1). Against overhand fastballers, a position toward the back of the box is favored. If the batter stands close and forward, he must hit the inside fast ball way out in front of the plate to prevent being jammed.

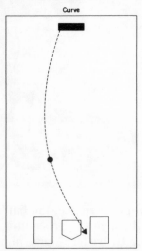

Diag. 3-1.

With experience, a player will determine which stance is best for him. During the early stages, however, it is sometimes helpful to assume a spread stance. This eliminates the early step and long stride, and helps protect against pulling the body away from the plate. These faults must be corrected in order to achieve success.

Hitting position: The bat may be swung back and forth or wiggled a few times to loosen the muscles before the swing. But, as the ball is being delivered, the bat must be brought back with the arms away from the body. Most batters hold their hands comfortably in front of their rear shoulder, with the forward arm parallel to the ground (Fig. 3-6).

Fig. 3-6.

Some coaches think that the front arm is the guiding arm and the rear arm the power arm. Others believe that the converse is true. Actually, it takes two strong arms to be an excellent hitter. Most players hold the rear elbow in a comfortable position slightly below the shoulder to help relax the muscles.

The hands usually are held at about shoulder height—the level that provides the *best* bat control in handling low and high pitches. Many boys wiggle the bat, allowing the barrel end to hang below the shoulders. This, of course, should be avoided. The bat, as well as the entire body, should be perfectly still once the pitcher begins his delivery.

Stride and Swing: In the stance, the weight is evenly distributed between both feet. As the pitcher delivers, the weight shifts to the back foot. The hips, shoulders and arms pivot back, the head remains still, the wrists are cocked, and the bat is cocked over the shoulder ready to move.

The actual weight shift to the front foot is delayed until the pitch can be determined. By turning slightly inward as the pitcher starts to deliver, the batter can help control his weight, enabling him to delay his step and time the pitch. This move also brings the wrists and body into the desired hitting position.

Some players do not delay their step in this fashion; they step early and, as a result, pull most pitches. Such players usually are outstanding fast-ball hitters, thanks to their early step. But they are usually weak against a curve or a change-up. Since some of their weight is transferred too early, their only power must come from the arms. The body weight must never be ahead of the swing.

The player who delays his step has no such weakness because he can hit to all fields. The batter should remember: step *to* hit, not step *and* hit. There is a big difference. If the batter does step too soon, he should keep his bat back in position so that he can swing at off-speed pitches.

In a well-coordinated swing, the weight is transferred from the ball of the back foot to the ball of the front foot. As the striding foot hits the ground, the leg braces, and the swing is made off this braced leg. This position permits the free hip movement so necessary for perfect timing (Fig. 3-7).

Fig. 3-7.

The swing continues with a forward pivot of the hips and shoulders, and a forward thrust of the arms, so that the barrel of the bat lags behind the hands until the wrist begins to roll out in front of the plate. The arms, which are kept away from the body, supply most of the power.

Once the batter decides to swing at the pitch, he should get the bat moving fast, and bring everything through smoothly, releasing his full power from his wrists and hands at impact with the ball. The wrist snap is the final accelerator after the hips, shoulders, forearms and hands have made their move.

The wrists should stay cocked until the hands reach the center of the body. Then, they should uncock with lightning speed. The wrists roll over as the ball is met well out in front of the plate (Fig. 3-8).

Fig. 3-8.

The head must be kept steady and firm, with the eyes on the ball. It should be followed from the pitcher's hand until it is hit (good pitch) or goes into the catcher's mitt (bad pitch). *The batter should never take his eyes off the ball.*

On pitches above the belt, the bat should be swung as parallel to the ground as possible. On lower pitches, the barrel end of the bat must be lowered. A downswing is preferable to an uppercut, particularly on high pitches, as it increases the chances of hitting line drives.

The speed of the bat also is a major factor. Many players employ a very hard swing, which often throws off their timing. A moderately hard swing, with a strong wrist action, is preferable. Ted Williams claimed that he swung with 85% of his capacity, but he tried for 100% effort with the action of his hands and wrists.

A problem for many a ballplayer is how to check his swing once it has been started. It occurs when the hitter has been fooled by a pitch or decides that the pitch is not in the strike zone. It is recommended that extra pressure be applied by the top hand on the bat the instant the decision is made not to complete the swing. This procedure has proven very successful at Lipscomb.

The Follow-Through should be performed naturally and smoothly without throwing the body out of alignment. If the swing has been executed on balance, the follow-through should also be on balance. Ideally, the bat should complete its arc at the middle of the batter's back. This indicates that the swing has been fairly level and full enough to assure good power.

An excellent follow-through indicates a good swing and permits a rapid break from the plate. Good hip rotation is needed to maintain balance in the follow-through.

Waiting for the Good Pitch: One of the secrets of successful hitting is swinging only at good pitches. Every batter has a certain type of strike pitch that gives him trouble. For some, it is high and inside; for others, it is low and away.

With less than two strikes, the batter should always take this pitch. It may be called a ball. In fact he should take any pitch that fools him (with the count less than two strikes).

The hitter should always be alert for the pitch that he knows he can contact solidly. When the count goes to two strikes, he should adjust by choking up—sacrificing power for bat control. This will increase his chances of getting a piece of the ball.

Since the player who swings at bad pitches is only helping the pitcher, the batter must know the strike zone. Experience and practice are the best teachers. It is very helpful to let the hitter stand at the plate against a pitcher and watch every delivery all the way into the catcher's mitt, with the catcher calling balls and strikes.

During regular batting practice, the catcher should inform the hitter whenever he is swinging at balls or taking strikes.

Most coaches believe that tension and overanxiety are the chief reasons for swinging at bad pitches. These faults may be corrected by having the hitter step out of the box and perhaps take a deep breath, thus giving him more time to get ready.

The batter should remember that as a rule he will get only four or five good pitches a game, and he must be ready for them.

Hitting for Power and Line Drives: It has been contended that solid contact is the main factor in achieving power. While this is somewhat true—the batter's primary goal should be to meet the ball squarely—it is not the whole answer to maximum power. Speed is also a vital element in hitting for distance. In other words, maximum power is derived from a quick arm and hip action and the rapid acceleration of the bat at the moment of impact.

Correct implementation and modification of the fundamentals will enable the player to hit with the maximum power afforded by his size, strength, and ability.

Most power hitters swing too hard. This affects their timing and balance, leading to frequent strikeouts. The consistent hitter uses a moderately hard, smooth, and basically level swing, featuring good wrist action. This type of swing will produce line drives and power hits, the ultimates in the batting art.

Hitting Various Types of Pitches: The batter nearly always must look for the fast ball. If thus prepared, he can easily adjust to the breaking pitch. If he is set for the curve, the fast ball can be thrown by him. Once in a while he can look for another type pitch, but this should be the exception, not the rule.

In certain situations, such as the start of an inning or whenever the pitcher is behind or having control trouble, the batter can definitely look for the fast ball. If the pitcher is getting his other pitches over but is wild with the fast one, the batter should look for the off-speed pitches.

For most hitters, the curve presents a far tougher problem than the fast ball. The batter should always *go with the curve.* If it is breaking away, he should attempt to hit it to the opposite field; if it is breaking in, he should try to pull it.

If a right-hander's curve is breaking inside to a right-handed batter, he can pull it. Usually, however, the right-handed pitcher will try to keep the curve low and away from the right-handed batter. In this case, the batter should step toward the plate and hit to right. The same theory applies for left-handed batters facing left-handed pitchers.

The batter should keep his front shoulder in as long as possible against the curve. This enables him to delay his swing and thus increases his chances of going with the pitch.

The batter must study each pitcher's curve, remembering that regardless of how much it may break, it is always slower than the fast ball. He must also remember that a curve thrown at him usually will break over the plate, and the one thrown over the plate will usually break outside.

Hitters experience difficulty handling the curve because (1) they have a strong tendency to pull away from the pitch, and (2) they do not follow the ball closely all the way to the bat. If they can break these habits, they can become curve-ball hitters. Another point to remember is that most batters cannot hit curves merely because they do not see enough of them in batting practice.

The change-up should be dealt with in much the same manner. The hitter should try to keep his front shoulder in and delay his stride as long as possible. An inside change-up should be hit straight away, not pulled.

Hitting in the Clutch: The highest accolade bestowed upon a player is that he is a "clutch hitter"—he comes through when the chips are down. The most uncomplimentary is that he is a "choke-up artist."

The batter must never allow the situation to intimidate him. He must convince himself that he will get the hit. He should never go to the plate with doubt in his mind. The greater the challenge, the greater should be his determination.

Mental Aspect. In addition to physical skills, the outstanding ball-player possesses the great intangibles of aggressiveness, confidence, determination, courage and concentration.

Though *confidence* alone may not make a good hitter, all of the great ones exude it. They honestly believe they can hit any kind of pitching.

Practice, desire, and ability build confidence, which, in turn, builds *determination.* Fierce determination brings out the best in a player, and it is absolutely indispensable in hitting.

Determination produces *aggressiveness.* The aggressive hitter is up there to hit. He expects that every pitch will be a strike and that it will be "his" pitch. This does not mean that he is going after every pitch. It does mean that he is ready and eager to hit, and that every time he swings, he takes a good cut.

All outstanding hitters have the ability to *concentrate.* When they step into the box, they shut out the crowd, the catcher, and all other extraneous factors. They concentrate on the pitcher and his weaknesses and also follow every pitch all the way to the bat.

The Guess Hitter plays into the hands of a smart pitcher. The pitcher knows what he is throwing; the batter can only guess. By merely varying his pattern, the veteran pitcher can put the guess hitter at his mercy. If the batter is lucky enough to guess correctly, he may hit safely; if he does not, he will look quite foolish.

As mentioned before, most coaches want the batter to assume that every pitch will be a fast ball, and then adjust to the slower pitch.

Though this author does not recommend guess hitting, he thinks it sometimes pays to look for a certain pitch in a logical spot in the strike zone. This wil depend upon the situation, the pitcher's habit patterns, and the batter.

When the sacrifice is in order, for example, the batter can expect a high pitch. In a double-play situation, he can look for the low pitch. When ahead in the ball-strike count, he can look for the pitch that the hurler is controlling best. If the pitcher relies mainly on one pitch, the batter should look for it.

Finally, in a tight game, with the pitcher in a hole, the batter can logically look for the man's best pitch. Most pitchers come in with their best whenever they are in a jam.

By watching the pitcher constantly—learning how he throws, what pitch he throws most effectively, and when he throws it—the batter will be able to *react*, not guess.

Major Batting Faults. Hitting is, basically, a natural skill, and it takes a gifted coach to teach it or improve it. The coach must possess a broad knowledge of the techniques and be able to recognize, diagnose, and, if possible, remedy the various weaknesses to which most batters are disposed.

Though some of these faults may not be entirely remediable, they can, in most cases, be treated. Both the coach and the player must be willing to devote considerable time, effort, and patience to accomplish this.

Following is an analysis of the most common faults observed in all types of hitters:

Overstriding: The batter stands with his feet fairly close together and then takes a long step toward the pitcher. Most batters do this to get their full power into the swing. This would not cause much of a problem if the pitcher threw the same pitch at the same speed every time. Since he does not, he creates a severe timing problem for the overstrider. Once the batter initiates his long stride, he cannot make any adjustments. Hence, if he does not get his pitch, he can be completely fooled.

Overstriders generally have difficulty with breaking pitches and changeups, since their stride and timing are set for the fast ball. Whenever a batter steps forward for a fast ball and then encounters an off-speed pitch, his weight is too far forward to assure good balance, making it difficult to meet the pitch accurately.

The remedy for overstriding is to widen the stance and take a short stride. This prevents the weight from going forward and provides good balance. With a short stride, the arms do the work in swinging, regardless of the pitch. It is sometimes helpful also to place more weight on the front foot, expecially in the early stages of the transition to a short stride.

Hitching: The batter drops his hands as the pitch approaches. This position forces him to rush his swing and to swing upward. The result usually is calamitous. Since he cannot level the bat as he swings, especially at high inside pitches, he will seldom get his share of base hits.

Many hitters drop their bat and then bring it back to the proper position before they swing. This, however, is merely wasted motion.

In practice the hitcher should concentrate on swinging from the starting position without any dip of the hands. He can also hold the bat against the outer part of his shoulder and raise his rear elbow. Practice in front of a mirror should help, since the batter will be able to see his mistake. The hitcher can also help himself by concentrating on keeping his hands as still as possible.

Stepping in the Bucket, a common fault among beginners, is usually caused by the fear of being hit. The inexperienced batter feels that he can protect himself by pulling his striding foot and body away from the plate. Though this movement may furnish some protection, it increases the difficulty of reaching the outside pitch.

Few hitters who "bail out" will ever hit for average. Those who have succeeded have moved their head and shoulders toward the pitch while pulling their front foot away from the plate. The average bucket-stepper, however, also pulls his body away.

Corrective measures have met with varying degrees of success. If fear is the problem, the batter usually is letting his imagination run away with him; if this problem is not licked early, it can intensify. Many coaches believe that once the batter is hit by a pitch, without any ill-effects, the fear will disappear. This, however, depends upon the individual's emotional make-up.

If fear is not the cause, the coach can help cure this fault by placing a bat behind the batter's front foot. Each time the player steps away from the plate, he will step on the bat. In time he should develop the proper habit of stepping forward.

Back-Stepping: As the pitch is being delivered, the batter takes a step back with the rear foot, then a step forward with the front foot. The first step is completely unnecessary. It throws the body off balance by moving the body-weight backward at a time when it should be steady and ready to move forward. *Cure:* The batter should place more weight on the back foot in his stance.

Head Turning on the swing causes the player to lose sight of the pitch as it approaches the plate. This is a common fault, often caused by over-swinging.

To overcome it, the batter must keep his head down and focus on the ball all the way onto the bat (if he swings) or into the catcher's mitt (if he takes). In practice, the batter should stand at the plate and keep his head still while following every pitch all the way to the plate. Another remedy for headturning is for the batter to imagine that he is meeting the ball with his shoulders.

Lazy Wrist Hitting: The batter, often one with weak wrists, fails to pull or whip the bat around fast enough. As a result, he usually hits to the opposite field, failing to capitalize on his natural power. Wrist and finger exercises—squeezing a rubber ball daily and weight training—should be prescribed.

If the lazy hitter does possess adequate wrist strength, the coach should have him practice swinging at a heavy object, such as a medicine ball placed on a stool. He must knock the ball off the stool, a feat which cannot be accomplished unless he puts sufficient strength behind his swing and follows through well.

Locking the Front Hip during the swing produces a substantial loss of body power. Whenever the rear foot is about twice as far from the plate as the front foot, the hitter's front hip action becomes limited. This position locks the hip, preventing maximum freedom of rotation. A limited hip action makes it difficult to pull the ball and cancels the value of the follow through. This type of batter should open up his stance or step toward the pitcher when he swings, thus allowing an easy, free body action with maximum body power. A good hitter has a loose, free, easy hip rotation.

Uppercutting, caused by a dipping of the back shoulder and hip, is a direct result of the modern home-run craze. Many would-be long-ball hitters would be much better off employing a level swing. Though a modified uppercut is not too bad on low pitches (though it usually will produce a fly ball), it is ineffectual on high deliveries, since the bat moves across the flight of the pitch.

The uppercutter should keep his front shoulder down and swing slightly downward on the high pitch. It might also be helpful for him to raise the back elbow.

Chopping represents the opposite of uppercutting—the batter swings down on every pitch. While this is desirable on high pitches, the batter certainly should not chop every pitch. He may be able to overcome this by raising his front shoulder and placing a bit more weight on his back leg. The batter's front leg should be kept straight and his weight forced into the swing.

Off-The-Heels Hitting: The batter is so anxious to pull the ball that he pulls his body toward his power field by lifting his toes and pivoting on his heels. This pivot action produces a faster bat action, which is effective on an inside pitch. But since the bat and the body are being pulled away from the plate, it becomes very difficult to hit any outside strike.

In addition, this movement away from the pitch toward foul territory results in a considerable loss of power. A good hitter keeps his weight on the balls of his feet (not his heels) and moves into the pitch.

Head Bobbing during the stride causes the batter to lose sight of the incoming pitch by producing an up-and-down image of the ball. This fault stems from an upward push off the rear leg in starting the stride. First the head is raised and then, as the stride foot drops to the ground, the head is quickly dropped. Steady vision is necessary to produce a clear image of the approaching ball. The batter should practice a short, low, smooth forward drive off the rear leg. The smooth stride and reduced body motion should result in minimal head movement.

Batting Slumps. Although no one has ever run a telethon for its victims, the slump remains the most dreaded disease in batting. It strikes without warning. The batter may be hitting the ball well; then suddenly everything will go wrong. He may feel no physical change nor notice any appreciable difference in his timing, but he just cannot seem to buy a base-hit.

Though its exact cause remains a mystery, a slump invariably results from some fault in technique. The hitter's timing may be off, he may be taking his eyes off the ball too soon, or subtly he may have changed his swing, stance, or position in the box. This change can be so slight that neither the player nor his coach may notice it.

Some coaches believe that swinging at bad pitches causes a slump. Though this certainly is a characteristic of a slump, it is not necessarily the cause.

Mid-season fatigue is a more likely cause. As the season wears on, the player becomes tired and cannot cope with the demands of the game. Tired eyes may not be able to follow the pitch quickly enough to contact it properly, and tired muscles may not respond quickly enough to get the bat around.

With guess hitters, slumps are inevitable. The odds on guessing right are loaded against the batter. When he guesses wrong for any extended period, he becomes frustrated and confused. His problem often becomes acute. He may find it difficult to swing without guessing, but he *must* adjust in order to eliminate the basic cause of his woes.

Emotional disturbances also can affect the hitter in judging the pitch and in swinging. Poor grades, girl trouble, home problems, or any number of outside pressures can prevent the batter from concentrating fully on the job, and without such concentration he cannot be successful.

Slumps often stem from injuries. If a player cannot grip or swing the bat properly, for example, his hitting is likely to fall off. Excess weight on the hips can also produce a slump. The "hippy" player has difficulty swinging the bat far enough forward and following through because he cannot roll his hips through early enough. He thus cannot put any power into his swing and tends to hit weakly to the opposite field.

Some players can worry themselves into a slump. They will go hitless in their first two or three at-bats and immediately begin thinking in terms of "slump." They are inclined to feel that the team's success rests entirely upon their shoulders. This type of player is mentally unable to stand the strain of daily play. Anyone who is "bugged" by failure in the early innings is unlikely to come through in the later innings.

The player who can forget a bad day at the plate is less likely to slump. He considers each game a new adventure in batting and takes his dry spells in stride, unlike the worrier who takes his previous failures up to the plate with him every time.

Unfortunately, most players cannot ignore any extended series of failures, and worry themselves into a loss of poise. They begin swinging at any pitch on the assumption that the more they swing the better will be their chances of hitting the ball. The result is total chaos.

Most coaches are convinced that a calm and intelligent attitude is the most important factor in breaking a slump. The hitter must not lose his confidence or composure. Anger, heedless swinging, and constant guessing will not improve his average.

Staleness is probably the most common cause of a slump. The athlete who is overtrained or who is exposed to a long schedule often will lose his vigor and alertness, both physically and mentally. The immediate prescription for this sort of slump is a few days of rest.

Though there are literally dozens of ways to cure a slump, the best prescription is the proverbial ounce of *prevention*. A thorough understanding of the batting process affords the best preventive medicine. A coach who can spot faults quickly and correct them can keep the hitter from becoming frustrated, thus preventing or at least shortening a slump.

Whenever a player does fall into a slump, some adjustments must be made, depending upon his individual needs and batting style.

Ty Cobb, for example, did not wait until he went into a slump. Whenever he was on a hot streak, he tried to maintain his physical and mental coordination by reducing his daily batting practice. This, he felt, preserved his energy and maintained his sharp mind-body synchronization, thus helping him forestall a slump as long as possible.

Hitters who are sharp enough to recognize immediately any changes in their style are better able to solve their problems and thus check a slump. They may change their grip, choke up on the bat, use a lighter bat, or shorten their swing to achieve the desired results.

It is generally known that many big leaguers adjust the weight of their bat to their level of strength during the season, mostly to prevent slumps. Early in the season, the well-rested player may use a 34- or 35-ounce bat. But as the season wears on and the bat starts feeling too heavy to swing quickly and effectively, the fatigued player often will switch to a lighter bat.

Another popular way of breaking a slump is to bunt as often as possible during batting practice. Bunting develops greater concentration in following the pitch and studying the strike zone, as the player must watch the ball longer. Bunting also places less pressure on the hitter and gives him an opportunity to relax in the box. This procedure is invaluable in getting a batter to stop chasing bad pitches.

Many slumps are initiated when the hitter starts taking his eyes off the ball a split-second too soon. *Tip-off:* The batter is swinging at strikes, yet is constantly missing the ball. Since he is taking his eye off the ball as he starts his swing, he is unable to make a last-second adjustment to meet a breaking pitch.

Additional concentration on each pitch—waiting a split-second longer—may help snap a slump. By watching the ball all the way to the plate, the batter can better follow any type of pitch and is more prepared to contact it solidly.

A hitter may possibly halt a slump by taking short, easy swings in an effort to hit the ball up the middle. He should try merely to meet the ball, not kill it.

Slump-ridden players should study the opposing pitcher from the bench even more closely than usual. The hitter should know the hurler's best pitch, his preferred pitch when he is ahead or behind the batter, and his general pitching pattern. This information will increase the batter's chances of hitting the ball well.

Many players change their hitting style when they are in a slump. This is all right providing the batter goes about it intelligently. Too many players make senseless changes in their frustrated state. They think that any change will be for the better.

When a hitter feels that his stride is causing a slump, he can take a widespread stance and not step at all in swinging. The spread stance eliminates the stride, cuts down the swing, substantially reduces body movements and jarring, and helps the hitter follow the ball better.

After the batter has resumed hitting the ball solidly, he can return to his normal stride and, in most cases, he will hit well. Note: In using the spread stance, the hitter must work his arms somewhat harder to compensate for the lack of power and motion ordinarily furnished by the other parts of the body.

Continuous encouragement by the coach is imperative. He should never show any sign of losing faith in the player's ability, regardless of how he may look at the plate. When a player must be benched because of a slump, the coach should discuss this with him fully and intelligently, attacking the problem from the hitter's standpoint. The coach should make it clear that the benching is only temporary. This will encourage the player to fight his way back into the lineup.

Wise handling has helped many a player lick a slump. A coach should never forget that a player can be made or broken by the manner in which he (coach) handles this problem.

POINTS TO REMEMBER

A good hitter should:

1. Select a well-balanced bat of medium weight and length.
2. Study opposing pitcher.
3. Be mentally and physically alert, but not frightened.
4. Have confidence.
5. Determine to hit the good pitch.
6. Watch the ball all the time; never take his eyes off it.
7. Think of nothing but hitting the ball.
8. Grip bat loosely when waiting for pitch.
9. Always be ready for fast ball.
10. Swing only at good pitches, always looking for "his pitch."
11. Know his strike zone.
12. Keep arms and elbows away from body.
13. Avoid overstriding.
14. Maintain balance and coordination.
15. Avoid lunging at the ball.
16. Swing the bat parallel to ground.
17. Step into ball, not away from it.
18. Avoid swinging too hard.
19. Avoid hitting off heels.
20. Avoid trying to pull an outside pitch.

4

BUNTING CAN BE TAUGHT

One of the chief criticisms of modern-day baseball players is their inability to bunt. The explanation is simple. Ever since Babe Ruth showed how easy it is to score with a single swing of the bat, the emphasis has shifted to the long ball. How many coaches devote enough time to bunting, and how many players practicing on their own will spend any time on bunting? Very few. Yet this valuable art is not difficult to master. All it takes is a little know-how and the right sort of practice.

There are two types of bunts: the sacrifice and base hit.

The Sacrifice Bunt. The batter's entire concentration should center on putting the ball down in the proper spot. To do this, the hitter must shift into position just as the pitcher's arm starts backward.

Several different shifts are available to the sacrifice bunter. The most common shift is the square-around, in which the batter turns toward the pitcher by bringing his rear foot forward to a point parallel to his front foot just inside the batter's box (Fig. 4-1).

The square-around has several disadvantages. Too many young players begin shifting their position while the pitch is being made and thus are unable to follow the flight of the ball. Also, in bringing the rear foot forward, the bunter will sometimes step on the plate.

At Lipscomb the players are taught a simpler (and safer) sort of shift; the batter merely pivots on the balls of his feet to face the pitcher (Fig. 4-2). This procedure does not give away his intention so quickly and involves less body movement, both distinct assets to the bunter. As the batter pivots, the upper hand slides along the bat to a position close to the trademark. It grips the bat very lightly, merely for balance, with the fingers underneath and the thumb on top (Fig. 4-3).

Some batters, however, feel they can secure better bat control by sliding both hands close to the trademark, with the lower hand controlling the bat. In either procedure, the bat is held well out in

66

Fig. 4-1.   Fig. 4-2.

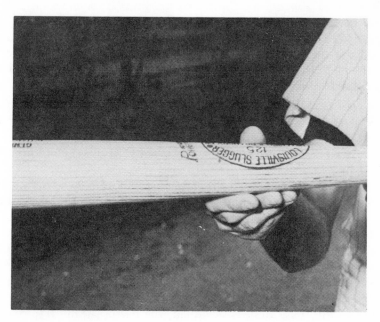

Fig. 4-3.

front of the body at the top of the strike zone. In this position, it does not have to be raised to bunt the ball. Any pitch above it will be a ball. The movement of the bat is thus always down, sharply diminishing the possibility of pop-ups.

The body is slightly crouched and slightly forward, with the weight on the balls of the feet, and the bat held with the arms relaxed and slightly bent at the elbows. The bat is allowed to give when it meets the ball, the impact making it recoil a bit.

The bunter should not push at the ball, but rather allow the ball to hit the bat. Neither should he pull the bat back as the ball approaches, a procedure which often produces a foul ball.

The ball is bunted by raising or lowering the body from the waist and knees with as little arm movement as possible. The batter's purpose is merely to "catch the ball on the bat." The lower hand (on the handle) guides the angle of the bat. A capable bunter can place the ball toward third or first by angling the bat toward the appropriate line with the lower hand.

The placement of the sacrifice depends on the pitch, the bases occupied, the defensive deployment, and the ability of the fielders. Unless the batter is an unusually skilled bunter, he should go with the pitch. The inside pitch, for example, should be bunted toward third base by the right-hander and toward first base by the left-hander.

With first base occupied, it is sound baseball to bunt down the first-base line. Since the first baseman must hold the runner close, he cannot leave the base until the pitcher delivers; he is thus unable to reach the ball as quickly as the third baseman. The ball should be bunted about 30 feet from the plate.

With first and second occupied, the fielding abilities of the pitcher and the first baseman assume larger significance. If the pitcher is the weaker fielder, the ball should be bunted along the third-base line. If the first baseman is the weaker, it should be bunted along the first-base line.

A team with a left-handed first baseman will usually be instructed to play for the force at third, since the left-hander can make this throw quicker than the right-hander. This bunt is also directed to a spot about 30 feet from the plate.

If the defensive team has the pitcher breaking for the third-base line immediately after he delivers, the ball should be bunted toward the mound. Sometimes the first baseman will charge straight in. If he does, the right-handed batter can try to push a bunt past him.

When second base only is occupied, the batter should try to bunt toward the third baseman. The idea is to force him to field the ball and thus leave the base uncovered. If the pitch is outside, however, the ball may be bunted down the first-base line. The throw to third would necessitate the tagging of the runner.

Pitchers are usually advised to pitch high and inside on the bunt situations. The batter should, therefore, assume a fairly upright position so that he will be above the ball when he bunts, to decrease the danger of bunting the ball into the air.

As a rule, the sacrifice bunt should not be used unless the runner or runners to be advanced represent tying, go-ahead, or insurance runs.

The Drag Bunt is a surprise attempt for a base hit as usually executed by a left-handed batter. He must conceal his intention until the last split-second. As the pitcher delivers, he slides his top-hand up the bat and takes a crossover step toward first with his rear foot (Fig. 4-4). He contacts the ball on the far part of his bat as he steps forward, and tries to drag it hard enough to the left of the pitcher so that he cannot field it, thus forcing the first or second baseman to do so.

Fig. 4-4.

The batter must start forward with his rear foot as the pitch is in flight, and the pitch must be a good one to bunt toward the right. If it is not a good pitch for this purpose, he should let it go or try to push it down the third base line. This may be difficult, however, if he already has started to lean toward first.

The right-handed batter's equivalent to the drag bunt is a bunt to the right of and past the pitcher, which forces the shortstop or third baseman to field the ball. This can be effective against a third baseman who is playing deep.

There are two ways to execute this bunt. First, the batter may drop his front foot back, push the top hand up a short distance, and bring the handle back toward the right arm (Fig. 4-5). Or, the batter may drop his rear foot back, slide the top hand forward, and push the bat handle toward the right armpit (Fig. 4-6).

Fig. 4-5.   Fig. 4-6.

Squeeze Bunt. There are two types of squeezes, the suicide and the safety. The *suicide squeeze* is one of baseball's most exciting plays. It is an "all or nothing" play usually employed with a runner on third and one out in a close game. With a skilled bunter, the chances of success are excellent, unless the opposition guesses right and calls for a pitchout.

The runner must not tip off the play by being overanxious—a common error in high school and college baseball. Since there is no need for more than a normal lead, the runner should not start for the plate until the pitcher's throwing hand reaches his shoulder on the forward delivery. If the runner starts at that moment, he will have no difficulty scoring on almost any bunt in fair territory. If the runner breaks too soon, the pitcher can adjust and throw an unbuntable pitch.

This also holds true if the batter squares around too soon. He must conceal his intention as long as possible. That means he should not assume bunting position until the pitcher actually starts to deliver the ball. The batter does not have to lay down a perfect bunt; all he has to do is to put the ball on the ground in fair territory.

On the *safety squeeze,* the runner waits until the ball is actually bunted on the ground before racing for the plate. He should move down the line on the pitch, but not so far that he can be caught off base if the pitch is not bunted. (If the pitch is not a strike, the batter should take it.) The ball should not be bunted too hard, and it should be kept close to the foul line. The safety squeeze requires a well-executed bunt and a fast runner.

It is very important for the coach to supervise the bunting sessions. He must make sure the proper techniques are used and must prevent the batters from becoming lackadaisical and careless in their bunting attempts.

The practice pitcher should throw from the stretch position and put some speed on the ball. It is a mistake to lob the ball in bunting practice. The deliveries should be close to game speed so that the batter can get meaningful practice.

COMMON FAULTS

1. Holding bat too close to body.
2. Gripping bat too tightly.
3. Not starting with bat at top of strike zone.
4. Not holding bat parallel to ground.
5. Pivoting too late, therefore not having body under control on attempt.
6. Dropping bat too soon.
7. Lunging at ball rather than waiting for pitch.
8. Pushing at ball.
9. Bunting balls outside strike zone.
10. Running to first before bunt is properly made.

POSITIVE POINTS

1. Hold bat out in front of body at top of strike zone.
2. Hold bat loosely.
3. Keep bat parallel to ground.
4. Keep head up with eyes on ball.
5. Keep body slightly crouched.
6. Pivot on balls of feet to face pitcher.
7. Catch the ball on the bat.
8. Get ball on ground before starting to first.
9. Bunt only good pitches.
10. Practice bunting.

5

AGGRESSIVE BASE RUNNING

Though everyone is not endowed with the ability to run fast, speed is not absolutely essential to good base-running. As long as a player can start fast and think quickly, he may develop into a skillful baserunner.

The smart runner is always alert to the possibility of an error, the slow handling of the ball, or an inaccurate throw. He knows which outfielders have the weaker arms and tries to capitalize upon their weaknesses for the extra base.

Upon reaching base, he assesses every possibility. He knows the score, the number of outs, the inning, the count on the hitter, the men on bases, and the strengths and weaknesses of the opponents.

The batter becomes a runner the moment he hits the ball into fair territory or the moment a third strike is missed or dropped by the catcher, provided first base is unoccupied and there are fewer than two outs. (With two outs, the batter may run to first base, even if it is occupied.)

Running to First Base. The batter should run out all fairly hit balls. Even though he appears to be a sure out, a break may give him a chance to reach first. Once there, he should never loaf. Loafing is a sure sign of a poorly coached team and a lazy ball player.

The ability to start quickly and get into running stride often spells the difference between a "safe" and an "out" call. The key to a quick start is a good follow through on the swing. Though the right-handed batter's swing carries him around and away from first base, his weight should shift to the left (front) foot. He should attempt to push off with this foot, throw his body in the direction of first, and take his first step with his right (rear) foot (Fig. 5-1).

Since the left-handed batter's swing and follow-through will carry him naturally toward first, he can easily cross-over with the left foot to start his run.

Fig. 5-1.

These techniques should be performed properly at every practice session. One effective way to work on them is to have every player run out his last swing in batting practice. He may run straight through the base or practice rounding the base.

Many batters, after taking their swing, will shift their weight back to the rear foot and push off this foot to take their initial step. Since this weight shift costs them a step, it should be avoided. If making a batter conscious of getting out of the batter's box more quickly interferes with his natural swing and affects his hitting, he should be instructed to concentrate on his hitting.

The batter must keep in mind only two things when leaving the plate: to run directly to first or to round the base. Since the bat-ball contact will indicate which of these to do, it is unnecessary to watch the ball continually. A batter can run faster if his eyes are focused in the direction of the run; also, he will be sure to touch the base. The first base coach will aid the runner also in making the decision to run directly to first or to round the base.

Thus, if the batter hits a grounder likely to be fielded by the pitcher, the catcher, or an infielder, he should run straight to the base without so much as a glance at the ball. He may run either to the inside or outside of the baseline, provided the ball is fielded in the diamond.

If, however, the ball is fielded near the plate or along the first-base line, where the throw will come from behind him, the player must run in the three-foot lane as prescribed by the rules. This works no hardship on the left-handed batter, as his start will be in foul territory. The right-handed batter, on the other hand, will start in fair territory, and he must remember to run in the three-foot lane.

On a straight run to the base, the runner normally will continue outside the base line. He does not necessarily have to turn into foul territory after passing the base. He may remain in fair territory as long as his path is a natural continuation of his run, and he makes no move to advance to second.

The runner should remember to step on the middle of the base and run beyond the base at full speed, slowing down gradually. He should not leap or jump at the base, since this is a slower method of reaching it, and in addition presents a great chance for ankle injury. The runner should slide only at first base to avoid a tag when the baseman has been pulled off the bag by a bad throw.

When the runner intends to round first base, he should, upon leaving the batter's box, bear slightly to the right and away from the base line, until he reaches a point at which he can turn and approach the base in good position to continue to second (Fig. 5-2). "Good Position" means facing the next base when rounding the bag.

Fig. 5-2.

A base-runner always should remember the shortest distance between two points is a straight line, and he should not waste valuable time and steps when circling the bases. He should touch the infield corner of the base in stride, using either the left or right foot. The important thing is to hit the base in stride (Fig. 5-3).

Fig. 5-3.

In rounding first, it is advisable to run without watching the ball until the base is reached. Once there, the runner should try to locate the ball and listen to the first base coach for instructions.

In making the turn, he should not be afraid to take a few extra steps. Some coaches teach their runners to go about a third of the way toward second. This places extra pressure on the outfielders and, if the ball is bobbled, enables the runner to advance to second.

The runner should develop the habit of rounding the base hard, always being ready to take the extra base if the opportunity presents itself. On a hit to right, the runner should not round the base quite as far, since the right fielder may throw behind him. Of course, if the batter knows he can make two bases, or if the coach is pointing toward second, he should continue without hesitation.

This procedure also applies to high flies behind the infield; a hard run and a good turn will enable the runner to make second if the ball drops in. The batter must be careful not to overtake a runner already on first base, as he will be out automatically. A similar precaution should be taken on long outfield flies, as the runner already on base may tag up in order to advance.

The coach should advise the batter on such plays. In some cases, however, the nature of the play will make it impossible for him to give any more definite information than "round the base." Here the runner must use his own judgment, make his turn, and proceed according to his running ability, the fielder's throwing ability, the score, the outs, and the inning.

Upon reaching first, the runner should remain on the base until the pitcher straddles or steps on the rubber. Since he must have the ball when he assumes this position, the runner's anchored position eliminates the hidden-ball trick. The runner should stand with his left foot touching the inside edge of the base, facing the pitcher and third-base coach.

At this time he should receive his sign, usually from the third-base coaching box. He must be aware of the runners ahead of him, the score, outs, inning and outfielder's fielding depths. Knowledge of the outfielders' positioning, speed, and throwing ability will help a runner decide how far he can advance on a hit, whether he should tag up on a fly ball, and how far to move off the base on an outfield fly.

Each time the runner returns to his base he should look for a signal from the coach. If he misses the signal, he should call time or signal the coach that he does not have a sign.

Lead Off First Base. The runner should take his lead by sliding his feet, rather than stepping out or crossing over. This will enable him to return quickly, if necessary.

There are many kinds of leads. Some coaches teach their runners to get far enough off base so they have to dive to get back safely. Others teach the "one-way" lead. Still others favor the "two-way" lead, which puts the runner in position to move either way from a normal lead.

In the "walking" or "moving" lead, the runner begins moving off the base a little later than in the other leads and keeps walking with short steps. If the pitcher does not force him to stop, his momentum will enable him to get a fast start for second.

The lead should be taken while the pitcher is receiving his signals (Fig. 5-4). The runner should not move while the pitcher takes his stretch. If he is moving toward second, he will be caught off the base if the pitcher throws to first from the top of his stretch or while coming set (Fig. 5-5).

Against a left-handed pitcher, it is usually wise to take a shorter lead. Since balks seldom are called on the left-hander, the runner must take extra care to see that the pitcher is throwing home before he (runner) moves toward second.

As a rule, every runner should make a good three- or four-step fake toward second. This sets off a chain reaction in the defense: The first baseman yells "He's going!"; the catcher gets set to throw, and

Fig. 5-4.

Fig. 5-5.

the short-stop or second baseman takes a step toward second. However, the runner must be careful not to move off far enough to let the catcher pick him off.

Regardless of the type of lead he takes, the runner should always keep his eyes on the pitcher and listen for instructions from the first-base coach. Good runners study the pitcher's moves. This requires diligent study, but the pay-off is big. They should watch the pitcher's right heel for the tip-off. If he does not lift his right heel, he is throwing home. The runner who knows the pitcher's moves can get a good jump toward second.

The runner should not attempt to steal if he is leaning toward first on the pitch, as he will be losing a step on his start.

As the pitcher delivers, the runner should break about two or three steps so that he can advance if the ball is hit on the ground or gets away from the catcher.

There is no excuse for a player's being picked off a base or doubled off on a ball hit into the air. The runner should make certain the line drive is through the infield before running. Even though it is a great temptation for the base runner to take off as soon as he sees the sharp line drive, he must wait until he is sure the ball is through the infield. A good infielder can make a great catch of a line drive and then double the runner off with a quick throw. This play, more than any other, destroys a team's chances for a big inning.

Base-Running Stance. After taking his lead, the base-runner assumes a crouched position with his legs comfortably spread, feet parallel, hands off the knees, and weight on the balls of the feet (Fig. 5-6).

Fig. 5-6.

Some players prefer to rest their hands on their knees, but most coaches want the hands to hang free. The only danger in this position is that the runner may lean too far forward and away from the base, preventing him from getting a quick start and increasing the risk of being picked off.

Whichever stance the coach prefers, he should check in practice to see that the runners are on the balls of their feet with their weight properly balanced.

The only time the runner should be permitted to lean is on the "one-way" lead. Some coaches advocate a short lead and a lean *toward* the next base for a steal attempt, and a long lead and a lean *back* toward the rear base if no steal is on. They think that the runner can get a quicker start if he is not afraid of being caught off base, and that a runner with a long lead will bother the pitcher.

Stealing Second Base. In contemplating a steal, the coach must consider the following factors: (1) Can the runner get a good start? (2) Can the hitter move the runner to the next base? (3) Is the steal worth the risk? (4) Does the situation make the play sound?

The ideal time to steal is with one or two outs, a right-handed pitcher on the mound, and a left-handed batter up. It is unwise to attempt it with two out and a weak hitter up. If the runner is out, the weak hitter will lead off the next inning. With none out, the steal may be sound baseball if the runner has an above average chance of making it.

The runner's first step should be a cross-over—a pivot on his right foot and a step across with his left. As he runs, he should not look for the ball; he should keep his eyes on the man who is covering. He will know which way to slide (away from the fielder's reach) by the way the man reacts to the throw.

Exception: If the pitch is hit, the runner should try to locate the ball. If he cannot, he should seek help from the third-base coach.

When the runner is going against a pitcher who is throwing with a stereotyped rhythm, he need only take a normal lead. He should start for second one count before the pitcher delivers. If the pitcher throws to first base instead, the runner should continue to second. Since the runner has a good start, it will take an accurate throw from first to get him. The runner should *always* slide into second on a steal if a play is being made on him.

Breaking Up the Double Play. In a possible double-play situation, the runner should slide into second in a way that impedes the relay to first. The rule states that a slider must have some part of his body within reaching distance of the base. This, in effect, gives him about three feet of sliding room on either side of it.

To break up the double play, the runner must slide hard and, if possible, hook the thrower's striding foot. By watching the second baseman in infield practice and noting how he makes the pivot, the runner can know on which side of the diamond to slide.

Note: With fewer than two out, the runner must be especially alert on a grounder to the second baseman. Too many runners allow the second baseman to tag them out and then throw to first for the easy double play.

The runner should never run into a tag on this play. If the second baseman comes at him, he should hold up and make the man chase him, delaying (or possibly avoiding) the tag long enough to prevent the DP.

Runner on Second Base. A runner on second observes a similar procedure. While looking for signals from the third base coach, he stays on the base until he is sure the pitcher has the ball. When taking his lead, he should carefully watch the pitcher and listen to the coach for instructions on how far to get off the base and when to return.

The coach's voice will help him determine whether to return all the way to the base or only part way. This can also be determined by watching the pitcher for a pivot move.

The lead off second differs from the one off first in that the runner can move farther off the base, as it is more difficult to pick him off. The big lead, which incurs risk, really is not necessary; however, the runner should remember that he is in scoring position. A four- or five-step lead is all that is necessary, as the runner can get a *moving lead* of 25 feet on the pitcher's motion.

The steal of third usually is an unwise play. The runner is already in scoring position, and the advantage of reaching third is not worth the risk. If the catcher cannot throw, or the runner can get an exceptionally long lead, the steal can be attempted, but only with fewer than two out.

A steal attempt with none or one out and a left-handed batter up is considered poor baseball. The catcher has a view of the runner and can get his throw away more easily than he can with a right-handed hitter at the plate.

The hit-and-run play is rarely attempted with a runner on second. It might be advisable with runners on first and second and a favorable count on a right-handed pull-hitter who consistently meets the ball. The infielders' movement to cover the bases on the steal could leave some big holes for the batter.

The runner on second should not be caught moving back to the base as the pitcher delivers. If the ball is hit, he will lose valuable time. If the ball is not hit, he should, of course, return quickly to the base when he sees the ball in the mitt to prevent any pick-off attempt by the catcher. This habit must be developed by all runners.

On a grounder to his left, the runner should advance to third. If the ball is hit at him or to his right, he generally should return to second. Otherwise, he can easily be cut down by the shortstop or third baseman. If the ball is hit slowly, forcing the shortstop or third baseman to charge it on the infield grass, the runner usually should advance to third.

The fast and alert runner can capitalize on any mental lapse by the shortstop or third baseman. If the fielder fails to look him back to second, he may advance on the throw to first. If the fielder does look him back to second, he should not advance unless the throw is bad or the first baseman has a weak arm.

On a short fly ball with fewer than two out, the runner should assume a lead which will enable him to return to the base if the ball is caught and to advance quickly if it is not. On long flies, he should tag up and attempt to advance if he thinks the ball will be caught. If the runner is on first, he should go two-thirds of the way toward second if there is a chance the ball will not be caught.

Going from First to Third. The runner must be aware of the outfielders' positioning and throwing ability and must discern how hard the ball is hit and where it will fall. If the ball is hit directly at an outfielder, the runner is unlikely to make third safely. If, however, the fielder must move to his right or left, the runner's chances of making third are substantially improved.

With two outs, the runner should be absolutely sure he can make third before attempting it. With one out, he can afford to take a chance. But with no outs, it might not be worth the gamble, since he might take his team out of a potentially big inning.

On a single to right, the runner should look to the third-base coach *before reaching second.* The coach will be able to tell him to hold up or continue to third. An alert right fielder might throw behind the runner, hoping to catch him taking a wide turn around second. Therefore, if the runner is held up, he should *stop on the base.* There is also the possibility that the cut-off man may cut the ball and trap the runner rounding the base at second.

Runner at Third Base. A runner at third follows the same routine as the runner at first or second. He should look for the signs from the coach since he could be involved in a delayed steal or squeeze play.

In taking his lead, he should not go more than a step farther from the bag than the third baseman. He does not want to give the baseman more than a step advantage on an attempted pick-off. The runner's lead should be in *foul territory* so that he cannot possibly be hit by a fairly batted ball (Fig. 5-7).

As the pitcher starts his wind-up, or delivers from the set position, the runner should start toward home. The distance he goes will

Fig. 5-7.

depend upon his judgment, but it must be long enough to enable him to get a good jump on a grounder, wild pitch, or passed ball, but not far enough to get him picked off by the catcher.

The runner must be leaning toward the plate when the catcher receives the ball. If he is caught returning to third, he will not be able to score on a grounder or passed ball. When returning to the base after the catcher has received the ball, he should move in fair territory (Fig. 5-8).

Whenever the infield is playing normal or deep, the runner should attempt to score on any infield grounder, unless it is hit directly to the pitcher. If the infield is playing in with no outs, the runner should hold up but be alert for a possible error. With one out, a fast man can attempt to score on a slowly hit ball or any grounder which forces the fielder to move and be off-balance.

The runner on third should tag up on all outfield flies and liners. If the ball falls in, he can score easily. If it is caught, he is still in position to score.

On short flies which apparently will leave the outfielder with a short throw after the catch, the runner should lead off the base. If the ball is caught, he should hurry back to third. If it falls in, he will be in position to score.

In tagging up, the runner should face the field toward which the ball is hit, with one foot resting on the inside edge of the base. His body should be crouched slightly with his legs comfortably spread and his feet pointing toward the plate. As the ball nears the outfielder, the weight should be transferred to the front foot so that the first step can be made with the back foot.

This technique affords a full step advantage over the "push-off with the tagging foot" method.

The return to third on any fly ball should become reflex action. Coaches must curb the player's natural tendency to move forward on all fly balls.

The Trapped Runner. When a runner is trapped off base, he should advance toward the next base as quickly as possible, forcing the defense to make a good throw to get him. If the throw clearly has him beaten, he should hold up and jockey back and forth to give any other runner a chance to advance. The more the trapped runner can force the defense to throw, the greater become the chances of a bad throw.

The runner should always try to work toward the next base and should run out of the baseline in a last-ditch attempt to delay the tag. Some defensive players will chase a runner even though he goes outside the prescribed lane.

The trapped runner sometimes can advance by forcing a man

Fig. 5-8.

without the ball to interfere with him. By changing direction just as the infielder makes his throw and then running straight at the thrower. the trapped runner may induce physical contact on the baseline. The umpire must call interference on this play and award the runner the next base.

When two runners are trapped, the back man should advance to the lead man's base and remain there until the lead runner returns safely. Only then should he attempt to return to his original base.

Inexperienced runners often leave the base too soon, enabling the defense to tag out the lead runner and then cut down the retreating back man.

Remember, when two runners occupy the same base, the original occupant is entitled to it. The other can be tagged out. Both base runners should remain on the base until the umpire signals one out.

POINTS TO REMEMBER

A good baserunner should:

1. Never call himself out; wait for the umpire to make the call.
2. Always run hard, regardless of where or how the ball is hit.
3. Watch the runner ahead of him.
4. Play conservatively, if the score is close.
5. Know his opponents; watch them warm up.
6. Slide into first base only to avoid a tag by a first baseman who has been pulled off the base.
7. Have his weight on the balls of his feet, and be sure to lean in taking his lead.
8. Remain on the base until he is sure the pitcher has the ball.
9. Never dance around while taking a lead.
10. Take his lead in a direct line with the next base.
11. Return quickly to the base after the catcher receives the pitch.
12. Know where the outfielders are playing.
13. Know the importance of his run.
14. Never allow himself to be doubled or picked off.
15. Be sure his weight is on his front foot, and facing the ball, if possible, when tagging up,
16. Avoid running into the tag on a grounder to second, when on first base.
17. Touch every base; it is there to be touched.
18. Slide into second base on all steals and double-play situations.

19. Make certain any ball hit to his right goes through before advancing from second to third base. On grounders to his left, advance immediately to third.
20. Be aggressive.

SLIDING, THE NEGLECTED ART

Perhaps one of the most neglected phases in teaching baseball is sliding. Many coaches fail to give adequate time and attention to this skill, and those who do concern themselves with it may not think in terms of what slide to teach or exactly how to teach each one. As a result, sliding is becoming a lost art.

There are four reasons for sliding into a base: (1) to avoid being tagged by a defensive player; (2) to stop the momentum of the player going into the base; (3) to avoid a collision with a defensive player; (4) to break up a double play. In a given situation, a player may slide for any of these reasons, or a combination of them.

Techniques for Sliding. Since sliding is controlled falling, the player learning to slide must first develop the ability to fall in a relaxed manner. To teach the correct body fall and other sliding techniques, the following series of drills are recommended.

The Fall: In teaching the fall, it is best to start the beginner in a standing position. The player stands upright. He then shifts all his weight to the left foot, which should be his take-off foot, bending his left knee slightly. He raises his right foot off the ground, bending the right knee so that the right ankle is inside of and extended beyond the back of the calf of the left leg, keeping the right knee pointed directly forward (Fig. 5-9). He then bends forward at the waist, bends the left knee, and falls on his left side, taking the shock of the fall on the outside of his left leg and thigh. The palm of the left hand is turned down as he falls, further shock being taken by the hand. The right arm is swung sideward and upward to maintain balance (Fig. 5-10).

The fall is executed on the right side simply by reversing the procedure. After the player gains confidence in falling from a standing position, he walks and then falls left or right. He should form the habit as he falls of raising the top foot and leg well off the ground, since this procedure eliminates the possibility of catching the spikes of the shoe in the ground.

Pit Sliding: When the beginner is able to execute the fall from the standing position, he is ready to go to the sliding pit and combine the fall with a run. In the sliding pit the player should gradually increase his speed until he is running at full speed as he goes into his fall for the slide. This practice will teach him to take off on one foot and slide on the opposite side, as in the hook slide. The sliding pit is used

Fig. 5-9.

Fig. 5-10.

primarily to teach the collapse to the ground rather than the body slide once the ground has been contacted. If a sliding pit is not available, the above drill may be done on tall or wet grass.

Field Sliding: After a player is able to fall correctly at full speed, he moves to the last stage of the sequence—actually sliding on the baseball field. Neither the fall nor the pit sliding permits much body slide. In the sliding pit there is some slide, but the sand and sawdust, while protecting a beginner, also slows down his sliding speed. Sliding into the bases on the field gives a player a genuine feeling for it, and the opportunity to experiment with the distance he should begin his slide. It is recommended that a small amount of sand be placed around the base where this drill is conducted and that the beginner wear sneakers or practice in stocking feet. Regular baseball shoes may be worn after the third stage has been mastered.

Types of Slides. *The Straight-In Slide:* This slide is used to get to a base as quickly as possible. The runner keeps his eyes on the base as he approaches it. If he slides on his left side, he should try to take off on the left foot and if on his right side, on his right foot. The straight-in slide is used to get back to the base on a pick-off throw or when the runner is in danger of being doubled up.

The Bent-Leg Slide: The bent-leg slide is usually made straight into the base. It is extremely effective as a brake and enables the runner to come up fast and continue on to the next base.

The take-off may be from either foot, depending upon which is more comfortable for the slider. As he starts his slide, the runner should fall back on his buttocks and tuck the take-off foot under his body with the knee bent at a right angle. The extended foot should be kept fairly straight and well off the ground so that the spikes will not catch in the dirt. The body weight should be on the buttocks (Fig. 5-11).

On an overthrow or mishandled ball, the runner can easily continue on to the next base, by hitting the base with his front foot and simultaneously pushing up with the leg that is tucked under him. His momentum will enable him to spring up and get away quickly.

The Hook Slide: The hook slide is used by a runner primarily to avoid being tagged. It enables the runner simultaneously to hit the base and fall away from the tag. It is important to master this slide on both sides so that the runner will always be able to slide away from the ball.

The slider watches the baseman's hands and slides away from the incoming throw. The runner should take off on his left foot when sliding left and from the right foot when sliding right. Both knees are bent, the left more than the right (when sliding right), and the feet are turned sideways to avoid catching the spikes in the dirt. The right

Fig. 5-11.

Fig. 5-12.

foot is brought forward and away from the base, while the bent left leg is dragged so that the toes hook the near end of the base. The momentum of the slide will cause the body to hook around to the side of the base (Fig. 5-12). In most cases the foot makes contact before the body falls away from the tag. This enables the runner to save valuable time which is often the difference between being safe and out. In some cases, it is necessary for the runner to fall away from the base before actually contacting it. This means that he will have to travel an extra step before arriving at the base, but the position of the fielder leaves no other choice.

The Head-First Slide: The head-first slide should be used only when a player is caught off balance and must dive back to the base or if the play is expected to be very close, and this slide will make the difference in the runner's being safe or out.

The slide is made on the front part of the body by springing off the feet, throwing the body forward, extending the arms, and reaching for the base. The reason more sliders do not use the head-first is because of the danger of being spiked in the hand.

POINTS TO REMEMBER

Before players beigin sliding, the following points should be stressed:

1. Never change your mind once you decide to slide.
2. Slide when in doubt.
3. Never attempt to slide with spikes on until you have mastered the fall.
4. Try to keep the hands clear of the ground to prevent jammed fingers and sprained wrists.
5. Never leap at the base; sliding is control falling.
6. Start a slide at least ten feet from the base.
7. Do not start the slide too soon or too late.
8. Concentrate on watching the base on the straight-in slide.
9. Concentrate on the hands of the fielder on the hook slide.
10. Eliminate all unnecessary slides.

6

GENERAL OFFENSIVE PLAY

The basic function of offensive play is to score runs and win ball games. To win, certain facts must be kept in mind at all times. They are the score, the inning, the number of outs, the strength and weakness of the defensive team, the strength and weakness of the offensive team, and the count on the batter. It is very important for the coach to be aware at all times of the state of the game.

The offensive strategy used by the coach will change from year to year as his personnel changes. When the team has strong pitching, outstanding defense, but not much hitting, the strategy is to play for one run. Other years when the team has good power but poor pitching, the play would be for the "big inning." With weak pitching the team will need several runs to win and should try to have the big inning in the early part of the game, bunting only during a late inning, if it needs a run. The coach must study his personnel closely to arrive at his offensive pattern. The ability of the players will determine whether the team is a running, bunting, hitting, or defensive ball club.

Some coaches will attempt to score one run early in the game, hoping this will somewhat limit the opponents' offensive strategy, since the opposition must score two runs to win. If the offense can score one other run later, this will require the opposition to score three times. Many coaches in high school and college baseball believe it is imperative to get ahead as quickly as possible and then play strong defense to protect the lead.

The question often arises, does a team play to win or tie the game in late innings? Games will go into the last inning with a team ahead by one run, and the opposition must make a decision if the first batter gets on base. Many coaches adopt the professional philosophy that the home team plays to win and the visiting team plays to tie. This is excellent strategy if a team is loaded with hitters, but in amateur baseball the percentage favors playing for a tie. Coaches must use common sense on their judgments. They should not expect their players to be hitters, if the records prove otherwise. Any coach should know his players and adjust his strategy to their capabilities.

The Sacrifice Bunt. The sacrifice bunt is used with no one out, the score close, and first base, or first and second base occupied. If a runner is on second base, he may be bunted to third if there are no outs and a weak hitter is at the plate. If this is done, he then can score on a long fly ball, an error, or a base hit.

The sacrifice bunt with a runner on first usually should be bunted toward first base, because the first baseman must hold the runner and will not be playing in on the grass. With runners on first and second and no one out, the best place to bunt is toward third base. This bunt should be hit fairly hard in order to prevent the pitcher from fielding it. If the third baseman is forced to field the ball, third base is left unguarded for the runner to advance from second. The same strategy is used when there is a runner on second base only, and the batter is trying to sacrifice him to third.

The sacrifice bunt should not be called when the team is more than one run behind unless the tying runs can be moved into scoring position.

The Hit-and-Run. The hit-and-run is designed to advance a runner from first to third base with fewer than two outs. This strengthens the position of the offense, since the team can score through means other than a base hit. The defense must be committed either to play in and give the batter a better chance for a base hit or play back and give up the run.

The hit-and-run is also helpful in preventing the double play, especially with a slow runner at first base. Every high school and college team should have one or two players who are capable of working the hit-and-run with some success.

The hit-and-run play is employed to best advantage with one out and occasionally with no one out. The batter should be ahead of the pitcher on the count. Such counts as three balls and one strike or two balls and no strikes are excellent times to use the hit-and-run. If the pitcher has good control, the first pitch after a walk is a good time to have the hit-and-run, since he will be trying to get the ball over the plate.

When first base is occupied and the signal has been given for the hit-and-run, the runner on first starts for second as soon as he is certain the pitcher has delivered the ball to the plate. The batter attempts to hit the ball on the ground and through the infield. If possible, he should hit it in the hole at second base or shortstop, depending on which infielder is covering second base. Most teams have the second baseman cover second base if a right-handed hitter is at bat and the shortstop if a left-handed hitter is at the plate.

When the runner breaks with the pitch, it is very difficult to get him going to second base, except when the ball is hit hard toward that base. Since one of the infielders will be moving in that direction to cover the base, he may have a play on the runner at second base. If the ball is hit to right field, the runner can usually advance to third base.

The hit-and-run play is sometimes used with only a fair hitter at bat with first and second bases occupied. Again the signal is given, and the batter attempts to hit the ball on the ground through the infield, making it very difficult to get a double play. The first baseman usually does not hold the runner on in this situation, enabling him to get a good jump on the pitch. The third baseman is forced to cover third base, which may leave an opening at his defensive position, if he moves too quickly to cover. However, with runners on first and second base and a good hitter at the plate, it is preferable to play for a base hit.

With first and third base occupied, the hit-and-run may be used in a situation when the count on the batter is three balls and a strike or three balls and two strikes. If the pitch is a ball, the batter does not have to swing. If the pitch is close to the strike zone, he should protect the runners by swinging to make contact.

In this particular situation the man on first base starts running with the pitcher's delivery to the hitter. The runner on third holds until he sees where the ball is hit. When there are no outs and the defense is in, the runner on third holds until he sees the ball go through the infield, or an error is made.

The runner on third may attempt to score on all ground balls except one hit directly at the pitcher with one out. If any of the infielders makes a throw to second base for a force-out, the runner at third attempts to score. The decision to remain at third or go home is based on the position of the infielders and the speed of the runner. If the infield is close, and the ball is hit sharply, the play will be on the runner at third, if he breaks for the plate. If the shortstop and the second-baseman are back in double play position and the play is made to second base for the force out, the runner should attempt to score.

The Squeeze Play. In the suicide squeeze play, the runner on third base breaks for the plate as the pitcher's arm starts forward to release the ball. Therefore the runner has an excellent start toward home plate while the pitched ball is approaching the batter. The batter must bunt the ball regardless of where the pitch is thrown, since a miss will probably result in the incoming baserunner being out. This play is usually called in a late inning, with one out and the tying or winning run on third base. A weak hitting team or one in a batting slump may play the suicide squeeze at any time provided it is not more than one run behind. A pre-arranged signal is given so that both the batter and the runner on third base know the play is on. In this situation, it is a good idea to have the batter return a signal to the coach and the baserunner so the runner at third does not charge toward home plate and then realize the batter has missed the signal. If the pitcher takes the set position, the suicide squeeze will work with a fast runner at third base.

The key to the suicide squeeze is the time the runner leaves third base for home plate. If he breaks too soon, the pitcher will be aware that he is going and throw an unbuntable pitch. If the base-runner waits until the pitcher's arm starts forward to release the ball before he breaks, the pitcher will be trying to get the ball in the strike zone. This gives the batter a better chance of getting a good pitch to bunt.

The double squeeze is attempted with runners on second and third base and one out. In this situation an attempt may be made to score both runners on a suicide squeeze play. As the pitcher starts his wind-up, the runner on second breaks for third, trying to get as fast a start as possible in order to bring himself as close to third base as he can. The runner at third base starts as explained above in the straight suicide squeeze. As the ball is bunted, the runner on second who has started for third rounds third base and continues on to the plate. It is best, if the ball is bunted to the first base side of the infield to make the second baseman handle the play at first base. In doing this, the element of surprise is used against the second baseman, who is primarily concerned with covering first base.

The Bunt-and-Run. In the bunt-and-run, the batter tries to make the third baseman field a bunted ball so that a fast runner on first base may advance all the way to third.

The runner starts when the pitcher makes his move to deliver the ball to the batter. He takes his turn at second and continues on to third base as the ball is being thrown to first. If the pitch is missed by the batter, the runner goes into second base as if the play were a steal.

When the ball is bunted to the third baseman, the runner making the turn at second base must be careful of a fake throw to first base and a real throw to second.

The Run-and-Hit. On the run-and-hit, the runner attempts to get an excellent jump on the pitcher, as in a steal situation. The runner on first should be fast, and he should play to steal second if the ball is not hit by the batter.

This offensive maneuver has many features that are similar to the hit and run, but differs in that the batter is looking for a good pitch to hit. It is not necessary in this play that the batter be a good right field hitter.

This maneuver is used quite often when there is a full count on the batter. The best time to use the run and hit is when the batter is ahead of the pitcher in the count such as two balls and no strikes.

Bunt for Base Hit. The bunt for a base hit is a surprise maneuver. It can be used against slow third basemen, slow fielding pitchers, and third basemen who play deep. It should be attempted by fast runners and usually when the bases are empty. It may be tried also when the offensive team has difficulty in hitting the opposing pitcher.

The push or drag bunt is an offensive weapon which creates many problems for the defense. Speed is necessary to the success of the bunter, and this maneuver should not be attempted by those players who are slow getting down the line.

Fake Bunt and Hit. In some bunt situations the defense presses the batter so closely that the possibility of success is almost negligible. When this type of defense is present, it is best to have the batter fake a bunt and hit the ball. He should concentrate on just meeting the pitch and hitting a ground ball. A good fake by the batter also may pull the second baseman toward first base, thus getting him out of position. The fake bunt and hit can best be employed early in the game or when the score is tied in the latter stages. The ground ball double play is seldom completed in this situation.

The Single Steal. Any discussion of the single steal usually pertains primarily to the steal of second base. This type of play is designed to move a baserunner into scoring position. In amateur baseball there are many opportunities for the steal because of the throwing inaccuracy of the catchers. Also, inexperienced pitchers enhance the possibilities of the steal. The stealing of any base is a gamble of an out against a possible run on a base hit.

A steal of third is relatively rare, despite its being more easily accomplished than a steal of second. The fact that the runner can get a much bigger lead and jump on the pitcher is offset by the fact that he is already in scoring position and need not risk an out by attempting to steal third.

A steal of third is best undertaken with one out and a right-handed batter at the plate. This advance will put the runner in position to score on a ground ball, a fly to the outfield, an error, or a squeeze play. Ordinarily, an attempted steal of third with no outs is bad strategy, since there will be three chances to score the runner from second base. It is considered unsound baseball to try to steal third with a left-handed batter at the plate, since the catcher has a clear view of third and can make an unobstructed throw to that base.

The Double Steal. The double steal is employed with runners on first and third or first and second. It usually is used to best advantage with runners on first and third base with one or two outs. In this situation the coach is gambling a run against an out or advancing a second runner to scoring position. The man on first breaks for second on the pitch. If the throw goes through to the base, he pulls up short and gets caught in a run-down. The man on third waits until the ball is past the pitcher before making his break for home plate. If executed perfectly, one run will score, and a runner remains on second base.

When there are runners on first and second, the best time for the double steal comes after one out. It is important to get a runner on third base with one out. If he is thrown out at third, one runner remains in scoring position at second base with two outs.

The Delayed Steal. The delayed steal is a play which should be attempted only by a base-runner who possesses both speed and split-second timing. It is tried after the catcher has received the pitch and only if the coach has noticed laxness by him in returning the ball to the pitcher or carelessness on the part of the second baseman and shortstop in moving toward the base after a pitch. If properly timed by the runner, he should take off just as the catcher starts his throw to the pitcher. The pitcher then must catch the ball and throw while the infielder who covers moves in from a deep position to make the play.

The Steal of Home. The steal of home is a daring but foolish play in most situations. It most logically is tried with two outs and a weak right-handed batter at the plate, when the pitcher has shown carelessness in watching the runner at third base. The possibilities for success are fewer at the higher levels of baseball.

The Forced Balk. In the forced-balk situation, there are runners on first and third base, two outs, and the bottom of the batting order coming to bat.

The runner on first base breaks full speed towards second when the pitcher begins his stretch. The pitcher must back off the rubber if he intends to run at the base runner. If he turns towards first with his foot on the rubber, he must throw to that base, or a balk should be called. If the pitcher does not balk, and the surprise fails, the runner should continue to second base at full speed. If a throw which beats the baserunner there is made to second, he should stop and force a run-down. On a throw to second or a run-down, the runner at third should attempt to score. It will take two good throws to prevent his scoring.

The forced-balk works most effectively on inexperienced and nervous new pitchers. The coach should not hesitate to use this play, if the percentages favor the element of surprise over the base hit.

Using the Bench. The wise use of the bench occasionally means the difference between victory or loss. Using a pinch hitter in order to have a more effective batter against the pitcher is an example. In making the substitution, the coach often will delay his actions until he is sure the rival manager has decided whether to relieve the pitcher or leave him in the game. This permits the coach to select the best hitter on the bench for this peculiar situation. If the decision is made concerning the pinch hitter before a change of pitchers, it may be necessary to substitute a second pinch hitter, if the coach has the personnel on his bench. Then the original pinch hitter will have been used without results and lost for the remainder of the game.

If the coach has only one outstanding pinch hitter, he should be used late in the game and when the situation is most crucial. The potential pinch hitter should have ample time to warm-up and have the game situation explained to him before he reports to the umpire. If a relief pitcher has entered the game, the hitter should study his motion, his speed, and his breaking pitches. If the pitcher shows signs of wildness, the batter should take a strike.

The substitution of a base runner at the right time may prove to be the decisive factor in a ball game. An astute coach forsees all game developments and always has the necessary players warming up, particularly in late innings when strategy is important.

SITUATIONS AND STRATEGY

1. Runners are on first and third base, no one out, and a pop fly is hit behind first. Both runners tag up, and the runner on first breaks for second as soon as the ball is caught. The runner on third starts taking a walking lead, and if the throw is made to second base he breaks for home. If the throw is not made to second, the runner goes back to third, and there are two runners in scoring position.

2. Runners are on first and third base with fewer than two outs, and a foul fly is hit behind the plate. Both runners should tag up, and the runner on first breaks for second. If the throw is made to second base and the defense does not have a cut-off man, the runner at third attempts to score.

3. When no one is on base, and the score is close or the team is several runs behind, the batter should take a strike. In this situation a base on balls is as desirable as a base hit.

4. Runners are on first and second base, no one out, and the score is close. In the early innings, strong hitters should attempt to hit. In the latter part of the game, the runners should be bunted to second and third base, provided the next batter is a good hitter.

5. A runner is on second base, score close, and no one is out. All batters should attempt to hit in the early part of the game. In the

latter part of the game, if one run is needed to tie the score or to put the offensive team a run ahead, and the batter is a weak hitter, the runner may be bunted to third base. This gives the next two batters an opportunity to drive in the run.

6. A runner is on third base with one out in a late inning, and the run is crucial. The coach may use the squeeze play if the batter can bunt.

7. Runners are on second and third base with fewer than two outs in an early inning. Both runners should attempt to advance on all ground balls except one hit to the pitcher. If the runner at third is thrown out at the plate, the offensive team has only lost one base. The offensive team had runners on second and third base before the play; if the runner is thrown out at the plate, they still have runners on first and third. This type of base running will put pressure on the infielders and score runs.

8. Runners are on first and third base with fewer than two outs. The runner on first base should never be tagged out by the second baseman after fielding a ground ball.

9. A runner is on third base with fewer than two outs. Generally, he will attempt to score when the infield is playing back and hold when the infield is playing in.

10. A runner is on third base with fewer than two outs and the infield playing in. On a ground ball to third base or shortstop, the runner fakes a return to third and at the instant the infielder releases his throw to first attempts to score. The first baseman will have to hurry his throw to the catcher, and it will take an excellent throw to get the base runner.

11. If a runner is attempting to steal a base, the batter can aid him by swinging to miss at pitches over the plate or by using the fake bunt. Sometimes this strategy will pull a defensive player out of position and also may bother the catcher in making a throw to a base.

12. If a runner is attempting to score, the player waiting his turn at bat should help by removing any equipment that is in the line of play. He acts as a coach at home plate, giving the signals to hold up or slide.

POINTS TO REMEMBER

The following points are important to the coach who is concerned with offensive play:

1. Employ an offense that corresponds with the talent of the personnel.
2. Give up an out to score a run.

3. Permit players to hit with the count 2-0 and 3-1 when runs are in scoring position.
4. Stress the importance of the sacrifice bunt, and practice this type of bunt.
5. Encourage fast men to bunt for a hit; this forces the infielders to move nearer the plate.
6. Endorse aggressive base running. It will pay-off in the scoring of runs.
7. Use the steal according to the speed of the runners and the situation of the game.
8. Use a simple set of signals that can be understood by all members of the team.
9. Encourage all offensive players to run hard on every play. The defensive team may make a mistake.
10. Use the bench, when necessary, to win ball games.

7

COACHING ON THE LINES

Coaching on the lines is an important phase of the game of baseball. The judgment and alertness of coaches at first and third base play an important part in the success or failure of a team. A base coach does not necessarily have to be very skilled as a player, but he should have a thorough knowledge of the game and the rules. He must also know the strengths and weaknesses of his own players and learn the opponents' as quickly as possible.

When analyzing the opponents, for bunting purposes, the coach should watch the catcher's throwing arm, the pitcher's motion with runners on base, and the strength of the third baseman's arm. He should know also the throwing and fielding ability of the outfielders in order to take the extra base against them. If the coach has never seen the opposing team in action and does not have access to a scouting report, he should observe its warm-up drills.

In amateur baseball, players are frequently required to act as first and third base coaches. It is advisable for such players to learn the routine duties of a demanding job which requires concentration, keeping one jump ahead of the play, and being prepared to make quick and accurate decisions as various situations arise. Regardless of who fills this role, he should understand thoroughly its duties and responsibilities.

FIRST BASE COACH

The first-base coach, although not having to pass judgment as the third-base coach, does nevertheless have important duties. He gives encouragement to the batter and once the ball is hit must help the batter-runner. If there is to be a play at first base, he encourages the runner to run hard and, if there is an error on the throw, signals hims to go to second or to stop. If the throw is high or wide of the base, he can instruct the runner to slide by voice or hand sign.

If the ball is out of the infield, the coach should move to the front of the box, point toward second, and yell either, "Make your turn" or "Go for two." He may wave his arm in a circle in addition to yelling for the runner to go to second.

If he has told the runner to go to second, the coach must watch the first baseman to see that he is not trailing him. Some teams have both the shortstop and second baseman to go out on relays, and a runner will round second carelessly thinking no one is covering the base. This play is used on a sure double and possible triple.

If the ball is called foul, the coach should move toward the baseline and hold up both hands, saving the batter as many steps as possible.

Runner on First Base. Once the batter reaches first base and cannot advance, the coach tells him to stay on the base until he can find the ball. This combats the hidden-ball trick. He also reminds the runner of the number of outs, the throwing ability of the outfielders, and their positions. If none is out, he tells the runner to play safe and not take chances. The coach should advise the runner to avoid being tagged by the second baseman if a ground ball is fielded in the base line, and to break up a double play if possible by sliding into the pivot man.

When the pitcher is ready to pitch and the runner has taken his position off the base, the coach sees that the lead is in the base line and is adequate according to the speed and starting ability of the player. He should also remind the runner of the pitcher's move to first base and of the catcher's throwing habits. Left-hand pitchers are extra tricky in throwing to first base; so it is important continually to warn the runner.

When the first baseman plays on the base, the runner always knows the position of the defensive man and takes his lead accordingly. However, the coach has the responsibility of warning him when the first baseman plays back. It is necessary for the coach to face the first baseman in this situation to prevent the first baseman and catcher from working a pickoff successfully (Fig. 7-1). The second baseman may also attempt to complete this play with the catcher when the first baseman goes in for a bunt. A catcher may attempt to work a similar play by circling down the base line after a ball is hit, and catching the runner after he rounds the base. If such a play is attempted, the coach must be alert and warn the runner.

Calling Fly Balls. If a short fly ball is hit with first base occupied, the coach calls, "Half-way" unless there are two outs. If the ball is hit deep, the coach can call "tag-up," for the runner frequently can advance. This, of course, depends on the speed of the runner, the number of men on base, and the throwing ability of the outfielder

Fig. 7-1.

catching the ball. If there is a runner on second or third base with first base occupied, and he tags-up, the runner on first is told to do likewise, for it is often possible to advance because of a throw to third base or the plate.

If there are runners on second and third base with first base occupied, they should tag-up, while the runner at first base goes two-thirds of the way down the line on deep fly balls. If the ball is caught, he returns to first base; if the ball is over the outfielder's head, he will score from that position.

The coach at first base must make decisions concerning short fly balls over the infield. The runner close to the play tags-up to eliminate being doubled off, and the other runners play off the base the distance the ball is over the infielders so they can advance if it falls safely.

All runners are told to tag-up on all foul flies.

THIRD BASE COACH

The third base coach has duties similar to those of the first base coach. In addition he has the responsibility of the base runner after first base has been passed. This includes indicating to him whether he should continue on to third base or stop at second. This is necessary only when the ball is hit to right field, because the runner is able to use his own judgment when it is in front of him.

The third base coach also has the duties of advising the runner when to continue on to the plate or to stop at third, when he should slide at third base, and toward which side of the base he should slide.

Aiding the Runner. Once the runner continues on to third base, he must be guided into it. If the play is likely to be close, the coach indicates to him to slide. To indicate the necessity of sliding, the coach should extend his arms toward the ground, palms down (Fig. 7-2). Holding the hands toward either side of the base will let the

Fig. 7-2.

runner know to which side the slide should be made. If the throw is exceptionally wild, or if no play is being made on the runner, it will not be necessary for him to slide. The coach gives the runner the stop information by holding both hands in the air, with the palms toward the runner (Fig. 7-3). If the play dictates that the runner should stay right on the base, the coach should point to it.

When a definite scoring opportunity presents itself, the coach runs to a point about halfway between third base and the plate, and faces the player rounding third base, meanwhile watching the ball so that he can judge whether or not the player can score. The baserunner is now the sole responsibility of the coach. If the player can score, the coach rotates his arms in a clock wise motion which is the signal for the runner to keep going (Fig. 7-4). In some instances it is advisable to yell to the player to take his time. This often happens when the runner can easily score.

Fig. 7-3

Fig. 7-4.

The position of the coach is especially important when the scoring opportunity is the result of a relay from the outfield or a fumble by the outfielder, because it permits the runner to be turned back even though he has rounded the base at full speed. As soon as the coach sees that the runner will have to be checked at third base, he runs back toward the base with his hands in the stop position. This permits the runner to return to the base without danger of being put out. The coach also runs back to his regular position in the coaching box after having sent a runner to the plate, because he may be able to aid another runner approaching third base.

In some situations the coach may want the runner to round the base and hold up. If so, he holds one hand in the air and points to the next base with his other hand (Fig. 7-5).

In order to make the correct decisions at third base, it is necessary for the coach to know the speed of his players, the throwing ability of the opposing outfielders, the throwing ability of infielders who act as relay men, and the defensive positions of the outfielders prior to the ball being hit. It is also important to consider the speed with which the ball reaches the outfield, the condition of the field, and the ability of the following batter. Other factors include the number of outs, the score, and the inning. A rule which is accepted by many third-base coaches is always to send the runner home from second on

Fig. 7-5.

a single to the outfield with two out because this hit may be the last scoring opportunity in the inning.

Runners on Second and Third Bases. When a runner has reached second base and cannot advance, the coach reminds him to "Find the ball." This also applies to the runner on third base. The coach gives the number of outs and instructs him to make the line-drive go through the infield if there are fewer than two outs. The coach tells the player to remain on second base if a ground ball is hit hard toward him or to his right with fewer than two outs. If there is a runner at third base, he is told what that runner intends to do. Of course, with all the bases occupied, all runners must advance on a ground ball regardless of the number of outs.

When a second and third base are occupied, the coach's philosophy will determine if the runners advance on a ground ball. Many coaches tell the runners to make a ground ball go through the infield before attempting to advance. This may be good strategy with none out and the infield in. However, with the infield back and one out, the runner should advance on any ground ball, except one hit directly to the pitcher. If the runner at third is thrown out at the plate, the offense has lost only one base. There would be runners at first and third base instead of second and third if they were held up. In a similar situation, with the infield back, and third base occupied, the runner is told to score on a ground ball hit to the right side of the shortstop and in some cases the third baseman, depending on where he is playing.

Another important duty of the third base coach is to watch the shortstop and the second baseman to prevent a runner on second from being picked-off the base. If both the shortstop and the second baseman play in their regular positions, the coach continually calls, "All right." However, if either of them moves toward the base, he yells, "Get back." The baserunner at second should concentrate solely on the pitcher, while the coach watches both of the infielders.

On fly balls, the third base coach follows the same rules as the first base coach. On short fly balls the runner plays off the base, and on long fly balls he tags-up.

The "on deck" batter is responsible for giving aid to the runner coming home, telling him whether to stand up or to slide. He should position himself so the runner can see him clearly. This is a very important job since it directly involves a run. Also, he should clear out the bat and mask if the catcher does not do it.

SIGNALS

Signals are generally used for five offensive maneuvers. They are the steal, take, sacrifice bunt, hit-and-run, and squeeze. The signals used should be simple and conveyed by a natural movement or gesture on the part of the coach. They can be given by one gesture, or a series of moves. They can be indicated by a key which precedes the sign. On some offensive maneuvers, it is advisable to have an answering signal from both the batter and runner. This avoids confusion and mix-ups in attempting plays. It is also advisable to have a sign the batter and runner can give the coach when they are not sure what signal has been given.

The signals for all offensive plays usually are given by the third base coach. Some managers or coaches go to the coaching lines and give all the signals. This, of course, simplifies the giving of signs. However, if the manager or coach remains on the bench, it is necessary for him to have a set of signals with the coaches to inform them of the particular strategy to be used. There are various ways to convey the signs to the coaches, as well as for the coaches to relay them to the batters and base runners. Any signs are workable if they are disguised. This is particularly true concerning signals given from the coaching lines, since the coach is in open view, and therefore a target for sign stealers on the opposing team. All signs are related to the coming pitch and are usually given after each pitch so that the coach may change his strategy to meet a different count on the batter, an advancement of a runner because of a wild pitch, or the failure of a batter to bunt the ball in fair territory. However, the sign may remain the same for the next pitch, in which case the rubbing of the uniform in a certain manner is often used to cancel the sign. It may also be necessary to take the signal off if the opposing team anticipates a steal.

Signals from the Bench. Signals from the bench usually involve one hand, which simplifies the work of the coach. The following set of signs shows how the manager or coach may relay the various signals to the base coaches:

> Touching the letter on the cap—TAKE
> Touching the face with the right hand—BUNT
> Touching the letters on the uniform with the right hand—STEAL
> Touching the peak of the cap with right hand—HIT-AND-RUN
> Touching the cap with two hands—SQUEEZE PLAY
> Folding the arms—DELAYED STEAL

Signals from the Coaching Lines. The previous set of signals could be used on the base line, but the base coach will need to disguise his signals, since he is in open view and a target for sign stealers as previously mentioned. There are innumerable gestures that can be used, but the simplest combination is the key series. The set of signals below shows this series:

> KEY—Touching the face with the right hand.
> SACRIFICE—Right hand to cap.

STEAL—Right hand to letters on uniform.

TAKE—Right hand on belt buckle.

HIT-AND-RUN—Right hand on pants.

SQUEEZE—Right hand to letters on cap.

TAKE-OFF (CANCEL)—Both hands on letters of uniform.

POINTS TO REMEMBER

The base coaches have a strong influence on the actions of the base runner, and they should keep in mind the following specific responsibilities which can help in this respect:

1. Do not allow the runner to take his lead until the ball is located.
2. Advise the runner of the number of outs and the game situation.
3. Advise the runner to take his lead while the pitcher is getting his signs.
4. Remind the runner of the pitcher's move to first base.
5. Watch for predictable rhythm in the pitcher's motion and inform the runner if a cadence can be "counted."
6. Watch the first baseman when he is playing back of the runner.
7. Watch the second baseman in a sacrifice situation; he may sneak in behind the runner for a pick-off throw.
8. Advise the runners what to do on fly balls and line drives.
9. Alert the runner on second if a fielder sneaks in behind him.
10. Know the strengths and weaknesses of your opponent.
11. Inform the runner when to take a chance or "play it safe."
12. Remind the runner at second to make the ball go through on the left side of the infield before advancing, if fewer than two outs.
13. Remind the runner to go full speed if there is a chance he may be forced.
14. Inform the runner as he rounds third if he should run hard or take his time.
15. Concentrate on other base runners after the runner passes the third base coach.
16. Alert the runner if there is a possible play on him as he takes his turn at third.
17. Inform the runners if they are going on ground balls or making the ball go through the infield.
18. Remind the runner at third to stay outside the base line while taking his lead and be alert for passed balls.
19. Inform the runner concerning foul fly balls, if he should try to advance or bluff a break for the next base.

20. Give all signals when both the batter and base runner are watching.

Part III

DEFENSIVE BASEBALL

8

DEVELOPING A
BASEBALL QUARTERBACK

In a baseball game, the catcher may be compared to the quarterback of a football team. He has numerous duties to perform, such as calling signals, directing the defense, throwing to bases, and keeping his team informed about the game situation, to mention just a few.

Players focus attention on him throughout the game. This means his actions and attitude can influence their thinking. The catcher must show confidence in his pitcher and strive to inspire it in his teammates. He can do this in many ways, often without uttering a word. Likewise, he can express skepticism by a mannerism or an action. A positive attitude by the catcher is very important in a successful baseball team. Needless to say, if he is doing a creditable job, he is the busiest player on the field.

Qualifications: Physically speaking, the catcher should have a strong throwing arm that is quick and accurate. He must be agile and must possess a sure pair of hands able to handle all types of thrown, pitched, and bunted balls. He must have considerable endurance, since the game requires more exertion from him than from any other player with the possible exception of the pitcher.

Many of the outstanding catchers have been physically large and solidly built, but there have been sufficient exceptions to prove that any kind of physique will do if a player has the proper attitude and can develop the essential skills.

In terms of mental and emotional equipment, the catcher should be both intelligent and dependable. He should possess a memory that enables him to recall successful and unsuccessful pitches thrown to certain hitters. He should make it a point constantly to study each batter to learn his weaknesses. He must always be alert for the base runners going and to all potential play situations.

Although he should be both mentally and temperamentally

aggressive, the catcher must also be able to surpress his feelings and remain calm under all conditions. Losing control of his emotions interferes with straight thinking and the ability to direct the ball club. The ideal catcher, in terms of temperament, is a rare combination of aggressiveness and drive with a capacity to remain relaxed.

Position Behind the Plate: The catcher's position behind the plate should be as close to the hitter as possible without interfering with the hitter or with his own receiving freedom. A good position is one from which the catcher can just touch the batter's elbow with his outstretched gloved hand (Fig. 8-1). There is little danger of interference at this distance, since the hitter's stride and swing will carry him forward. This close position also allows the umpire better visibility for his call, especially on pitches around the knees, gives the pitcher a better target, and helps the catcher handle foul tips, or low pitches more easily.

Fig. 8-1.

Giving Signals: The catcher's position in giving signals is a full squat from which he can survey the diamond and evaluate the situation. Giving signals is one of the catcher's arts which is sometimes underestimated. Signals are the language of the baseball field through which players communicate with each other. Those used by the catcher determine the whole defensive pattern of the game. They must be clear and simple enough to be read easily, but at the same time they must not be given in such a manner that the opposition can pick them up. Special attention should be paid to the arm and elbow, which can reveal signals unless held in the same position each time a signal is flashed. It is important that the shortstop and the second baseman read the signals, so they may be relayed to the outfielders. The first and the third baseman should check the catcher's signals from time to time, and if they can see them, the fact should be reported. A fair degree of precaution can protect the simplest of signals from detection.

There are many ways in which the catcher can give signals to his pitcher. They may be given with the right hand on the inside of the leg, well hidden in the crotch. They may be given also with the glove, and with the hands outside the crotch. Regardless of what system is used, the catcher should take a squat position behind the plate, with his feet spread comfortably, his knees apart, and the left forearm resting on the left thigh, with the glove extended beyond the knee (Fig. 8-2).

The simplest and most common type of signals used in baseball is the single series. A sample of this method is one finger indicating a fast ball, two fingers showing a curve, and three fingers, a change of pace. Four and five fingers could be used to indicate other pitches or a pitchout.

Fig. 8-2.

In the glove series, the forearm rests on the left thigh, with the mitt extended over the knee as false signals are given in the crotch. The wrist of the mitt hand hangs loosely over the knee. When the thumb side of the catcher's mitt is pointed squarely at the pitcher, a fast ball is indicated; when the palm side of the mitt shows, a curve ball is signaled; when the back of the mitt is facing the pitcher, a change is indicated; when the thumb of the mitt is up, a pickout is wanted. The glove series is excellent for night games, when it is difficult to see the single series in the crotch.

The multiple series is somewhat more complicated than the two previously mentioned. The catcher gives three consecutive signals with his fingers, and the prearranged one is the pitch to be thrown. For example, the second signal may be the prearranged sign, and the pitcher will disregard the first and third signals given. Another way of using the mulitiple series is to have an indicator given first to tell the pitcher which of the next signals is the pitch. For example, if he flashes two fingers first, then the pitcher uses the second sign of the next series given as the pitch. If one finger indicates a fast ball, the following would be the signal for that pitch: 2-3-1-2.

In the combination series, the catcher uses some part of his catching gear in conjunction with his fingers. For example, the position of his mitt may indicate a certain number which should be added to the number given in the crotch to determine which pitch should be thrown. The mitt resting on the thigh may be one, the mitt hanging loosely over the knee is two, and the mitt in any other position would be three. These numbers then are added to the number of fingers in the crotch to arrive at the signals, which would be four, a fast ball, five, a curve, and six, a change of pace. If the mitt is indicating two and there are two fingers signalling in the crotch, this would make four, which means a fast ball. These signals are so difficult to steal they practically eliminate the problem of changing signals every time a man gets on second.

After the signals for the type of pitch, the catcher should give another sign, indicating where it should be thrown, high or low, inside or out. The signal in Figure 8-3 shows the sign for a low pitch. The catcher may place his hand against the upper thigh to indicate inside or outside, depending on the side from which the batter hits. *Catching Position:* The position into which the catcher moves after giving the signal depends on the pitcher and the game situation. If the pitcher is a control or curve ball artist, most of his pitches will be low, and the catcher would assume a low, relaxed position. He may wish to move his feet farther apart as he crouches to receive the pitch or even drops to one knee. In this position he must be alert for a bunt, for which he is now more vulnerable.

If the pitcher depends on a fast ball which is often high, the

Fig. 8-3.

catcher should obviously assume a more upright position. When handling a pitcher who is wild, the catcher should always be in a fairly upright position, being careful to remain stationary during the pitcher's windup.

When runners are on base, the catcher must maintain a more erect position, so he will be ready to throw. His feet are spread, and he assumes a "heel and toe" alignment. The left foot is placed in front of the right by about six inches, so the heel of the left foot is opposite the toe of the right foot (Fig. 8-4). The right foot should be pointed outward slightly towards first base to facilitate shifting and throwing.

The catcher should keep his hands and arms relaxed and extended forward. A common mistake for catchers is to have their elbows between their legs in giving the target. This handicaps their ability to move the mitt to receive the ball properly. Del Crandall, a great defensive catcher, says "The catcher must take charge of the ball after it is thrown and not let the ball take charge of him." This relates mainly to breaking pitches. If the catcher lets the ball take charge of him, the strike on the corner is going to look like a ball to the umpire. The catcher should meet the ball with his mitt and catch it firmly before it breaks out of the strike zone. An important point here is for the catcher to catch the ball on the corner of the plate with his mitt to the side (Fig. 8-5), rather than up or down (Fig. 8-6). If he is doing a good job, the strike that is close to being a ball

Fig. 8-4.

Fig. 8-5.

Fig. 8-6.

will look more like a strike than a ball. The catcher is not cheating; he is making sure the umpire gets a good look at the pitch when it passes through the strike zone by stopping the ball there.

The catcher should keep his bare hand against the back of the mitt and place it over the ball after it strikes the mitt. This helps eliminate the possibility of injury to the hand or fingers from foul tips. Another method catchers often use is to keep the finger loosely closed around the thumb (Fig. 8-7). The fist should not be clenched, and the hand should be relaxed. As the ball strikes the glove, the bare hand is placed over it. No catcher can avoid getting hit on the hand with a foul tip occasionally, but he will rarely sustain anything more serious than a painful bruise, if he uses the above technique.

BASIC DEFENSIVE PLAYS

Dropped Third Strike: When first base is unoccupied and the catcher drops a third strike, he should always try to tag the batter after retrieving the ball. If there is no chance of tagging the runner, he should throw to first base. This should also be done with first base occupied and two outs. If there are fewer than two outs and first base is occupied, the batter-runner is automatically out. When the bases are loaded with two outs, the catcher should step on home plate for the force-out instead of throwing the ball.

No One On Base: When a ground ball is hit and fielded in the in-field, the catcher should back up the throw to first base. If the throw

Fig. 8-7.

comes from the second baseman, he backs up directly behind the throw. If it comes from the left side of the infield, he should go as far as he can, realizing he cannot get in a direct line with the throw. The right fielder should be moving in to help out. The catcher should be alert to balls that may be deflected in his direction or overthrows that may bounce off the wall or fence behind first base.

Runner on First Base: When a ground ball is hit to the infield, the catcher should hold his position until he is sure the force-out is made at second base. He then moves in the direction of first base. If the ball is bunted along the third base line and the third baseman fields it, the catcher should cover third base, if another player does not do so. This will prevent the runner advancing from first to third on the bunt. While the catcher is moving toward third base, he should call to the third baseman to cover home plate.

Receiving Throws from the Outfielders: When the catcher is receiving throws from the outfielders, he must make every effort to catch the ball first and then tag the runner the best possible way. Since many of the throws are not accurate, he must make whatever adjustment is necessary for the tag. If possible, the catcher should always tag low.

It is not wise for the catcher to attempt deliberately to block home plate unless the runner slides. If he does slide, the catcher should drop to one or both knees and brace himself. He should tag the runner with the ball in both hands, whenever possible, gripping it very tightly in the right hand (Fig. 8-8). If this is done, in case the mitt is knocked from the catcher's left hand, he still has the ball in his right hand. It should be pointed out that the catcher cannot block the plate without possession of the ball.

The catcher should give the outfielders good targets by lining up the cut-off men correctly and by placing himself in the proper position.

Fig. 8-8.

On a ball thrown in from the right field side of the diamond, the catcher should stand four or five inches from the third base line in foul territory and close to the plate. Both feet should be parallel to the third base line and on the third base side of home plate, facing the throw (Fig. 8-9). This position places the plate in front of the catcher and leaves it in full view of the base runner. Under these conditions the runner will normally slide to the infield side of the diamond. As the catcher takes the throw, he drops to one or both knees and makes the tag as the runner slides for the plate.

If the throw comes from the left field side, the catcher should place his feet parallel to the first base line, close to the front edge of the plate, and face the throw (Fig. 8-10). The base runner will

Fig. 8-9.

Fig. 8-10.

normally slide to the foul territory side of the plate, since it is open to that side. As the catcher makes the catch, he drops to either or both knees, keeping his bare hand well-covered in the glove to protect it, and tags the runner.

In receiving throws from centerfield, the catcher is in a position similar to that described from left field except he is more nearly in front of the plate and facing in that direction (Fig. 8-11).

Fig. 8-11.

In making the catch, he should not reach for the ball too soon, if the throw is an accurate one. If he keeps his arms at his side until the last possible moment, he can often trick the runner into slowing up slightly because he assumes there is no play. On a close play, this decoy device may be the difference between a run and an out.

On all throws wide of the plate, the catcher leaves his position and catches or blocks the ball so that no other base runner can advance. If there is a play after he has secured the ball, he should dive for the third base side of the plate. When the throw is late and he has no play at home, he should call to the cutoff man to take the throw. At the same time he should step into the diamond and out of the runner's way. If the cutoff man can make a play at another base, the catcher should call it.

Throwing by the Catcher: In most situations it is desirable for the catcher to use the snap over-hand throw, which has good carry and is faster than the full arm overhand.

Since the catcher must be able to throw quickly and accurately to any base, he must be able to execute all types of throws. For example, if a ball is bunted or hit in front of home plate, and he must hurry his throw to first or third base, he may use a sidearm or underhand snap without raising the body, but because of the distance to second base, he should use the overhand throw. Generally speaking, a catcher who gets rid of the ball quickly and accurately is more effective than one who throws hard but gets rid of the ball slowly.

If a catcher is having difficulty in throwing accurately, the coach usually will find the fault in the placement of his feet and his balance. The basic position for any type of throwing when speed and accuracy are required is the balance on the right foot, with the left foot used as a guide. The catcher should develop the habit of throwing off the right foot.

The mechanics of throwing include proper grip of the ball, coordinated arm and body movements, and the follow-through. The ball should be gripped across the seams so that it will rotate directly backwards. This type of rotation will give it more carry and more accuracy.

As the catcher receives the ball, the right hand moves over it, and the fingers feel for the seams. The mitt and the ball move back toward the right shoulder as the catcher shifts his weight to his right foot. The ball is taken from the mitt before it reaches the shoulder and is cocked up over the ear as the hip and shoulder rotate. It is important to have the elbow as high as the shoulder for maximum power behind the throw.

The catcher starts his throw when he shifts his weight from the right foot to the left in the direction of the target. As the ball is released, all weight should be on the left foot, with the right foot coming forward on the follow-through. The wrist should snap straight downward as the ball is released.

Shifting by the Catcher: In receiving the ball, the catcher should keep his body in front of the pitch as much as possible, by shifting quickly with the foot nearer the ball. The shift should be made with the fewest possible number of steps to conserve time.

The catcher should not reach for the pitch or receive the ball flat-footed. Being a "reacher" is not consistent with outstanding catching. He should learn to shift his feet properly and get in front of every pitch whenever possible. "Reachers" have a high precentage of passed balls and missed third strikes. In shifting, the catcher will have greater success if he keeps his weight on his toes and moves his feet before moving his body.

It is important for the catcher to shift so that he is in throwing position immediately after receiving the pitch. If it is over the plate, he should shift his weight to his right foot, ready to throw to any base. This procedure can be speeded up by his taking a short step forward with the right foot as the hitter swings, being careful not to interfere with his swing. The right foot should hit the ground just as the ball hits the mitt.

If a righthanded hitter is at the plate and the pitch is outside, the catcher should step to the right with the right foot and step forward with the left foot to make the throw to any base.

On pitches which are not very far inside to a righthanded hitter, the catcher should not move his left foot, but should take a short step forward with the right foot as he receives the ball. He can get the throw away faster by using this footwork (Fig. 8-12).

Fig. 8-12.

On pitches which are too far inside to handle easily with this method, the catcher should step left and slightly forward with his left foot to receive the pitch, and then forward with his right foot. After the right foot is moved forward, the stride to throw is made with the left foot.

If the pitch is inside to a left-handed hitter, the catcher usually steps to the right and slightly forward with the right foot to receive the pitch and then can throw in front of or over the hitter, who has pulled or ducked away from the plate.

Most catchers have trouble throwing to third base with a right-handed hitter at bat, expecially on pitches inside. On a pitch to his left, the catcher takes his initial step to the left, and then swings his right foot diagonally backward behind his left foot. He then steps toward third base with his left foot for the throw, which is behind the batter, if he does not move. With a right-handed hitter at the plate, if the pitch is away but not too wide, the catcher steps to the right for the catch and then shifts his weight back to the left foot. He then should step diagonally back of the left foot, shifting his weight to the right, and step out with his left foot for the throw to third base.

This throw can also be made in front of the batter if the catcher steps diagonally forward with the right foot as he makes the catch. The batter's position in the box, of course, may affect this.

The catcher should keep in mind that all shifts must be made while keeping the body in good balance and in position to make the throw.

Catching Fly Balls: All fly balls in the area of home plate which can be handled by the first or the third baseman should be caught by them, since this is a very difficult play for the catcher.

The catcher should know that if a right-handed batter fouls off an inside pitch or a left-handed hitter an outside pitch, he should start back to his left. If a right-handed batter fouls off an outside pitch or a left-handed hitter an inside pitch, he should start back to his right.

As soon as the ball is hit into the air and the catcher sees he has a chance to handle it, he should remove his mask. He should hold it until he locates the ball and then toss it in the opposite direction to which he is moving (Fig. 8-13).

The catcher should remember that a foul fly ball will always curve toward the outfield because of the rotation of the ball, provided no wind is blowing. If the catcher's back is to the infield in catching a foul fly ball, he should play it arm's length in front of him, since it will curve back toward him. The higher the fly, the greater the curve.

If a strong wind is blowing from the outfield, it will eliminate the curve, but if it is blowing toward the outfield, the curve will be greater, and the ball must be played accordingly. Whenever possible the catcher should try to have his back to the outfield on pop fly balls, so that the ball will be curving toward him. Most professional catchers state it is easier to handle the fly ball curving toward them than one curving away.

Since most fly balls do curve when they come down, the catcher will find them easier to handle if he holds his hands high and close to his chest, with the palms up and the fingers pointing away (Fig. 8-14). In this position, he does not block his view with the mitt, and if the ball is not caught cleanly, he will have a better chance of holding it by drawing the hands toward the chest.

Fig. 8-13.

Fig. 8-14.

Blocking Low Pitches: When falling to block pitches, the catcher should keep his body facing the ball so it will drop in front of him. On balls to the right, he draws in the left leg and squares the mitt with the ball by bringing his left elbow in close to his body (Fig. 8-15).

Fig. 8-15.

High bounces which hit in front of or beside the plate are played by holding the arms down and against the body. The ball usually will rebound a few feet in front of home plate.

Low bounces are played by the catcher's dropping down on one or both knees, placing the glove near the ground facing the ball, and trying to catch or block it with the mitt.

Fielding Bunts: When a ball is bunted in the catcher's area, he should start for it quickly. The catcher can get a faster start if he raises his body a little higher and places his right foot a little farther back while in the receiving stance.

As he moves out for the bunt, he should flip off his mask in the opposite direction to which he is going. If the ball is bunted down the third base line and the throw is to first base, he may field it with his body to the right of the ball and his back toward first base (Fig. 8-16). On a rolling ball, he should place the left foot as close to the ball as possible, so that he has plenty of space to field it as it rolls to his right. If it has stopped rolling, he places his right foot close to the ball, makes a turn to his left on his right foot, and then steps out with his left foot as he throws to first base. This method of fielding a ball down the third base line helps the catcher maintain his balance.

Fig. 8-16.

Some coaches teach that the catcher should circle to the left of the ball to make the play to first base (Fig. 8-17). This method is acceptable but slower. If there is a possible throw to second or third base, he should keep the ball in front of him. Even though circling to the left of the ball is slower, most amateur catchers are more likely to make an accurate throw if they are facing the play.

If the ball is bunted down the first base line and the throw is to go to first base, the catcher approaches the ball from the left side. If the throw is to second base, he runs straight at the ball. In fielding the bunt, he should place the gloved hand in front of the ball and scoop it into his mitt with the throwing hand, while remaining in a crouched position (Fig. 8-18). He should use the bare hand only if the ball has stopped rolling, and it is a "do or die" play. If he has time, he should use the snap overhand throw.

Bunted balls along either base line should be permitted to roll, whenever the batter-runner cannot be thrown out at first base. If the ball rolls foul, it should immediately be touched, so it will not roll fair. If another base is occupied, the catcher must be alert that the base runner does not advance an extra base if the ball does not roll foul.

Batter Weaknesses: In working with the pitcher, the catcher will

Fig. 8-17.

Fig. 8-18.

find some weaknesses common to almost all batters. The weakness is that pitch which the batter does not hit well. A right-handed pitcher pitching to a right-handed batter usually will find him weak on one of the following pitches: a high fast ball inside, a low fast ball outside, or a curve ball low and away. When a right-handed pitcher is pitching to a left-handed batter, the catcher will find him weak on a fast ball low and outside or a curve ball low and inside.

When a left-handed pitcher is pitching to a right-handed batter, he usually will find him weak on a fast ball low and outside, a curve ball inside and on the knees, or a fast ball high and outside. When a left-handed pitcher is pitching to a left-handed batter, the catcher usually will find him weak on a curve ball low and outside, a fast ball high and inside, or a fast ball low and outside. There are always exceptions, but these general principles do apply.

A right-handed batter who pulls the ball into left field usually hits an inside pitch well. The catcher should signal for a low outside pitch, either a fast ball or a curve. If he is a right-handed batter and hits everything to right field, he usually likes the outside pitch and probably swings late. The signal should be for a high inside pitch, since this type of batter will have difficulty getting around in time to meet the ball squarely. If the batter is left-handed and pulls the ball into right field consistently, he should be pitched low and outside. If he hits into left field consistently, in all probability he will have trouble with the high and inside pitch.

The straight-away hitter may be expected to hit to either field, unless he shows other faults. It usually is preferable to keep the ball away from him, whether a curve or a fast ball, with occasionally a change of pace to keep him off balance.

Spotting Batting Weaknesses: Some batters have batting habits which prevent them from hitting some types of pitches well, and it is important for both the pitcher and the catcher to spot such characteristics and to capitalize upon them.

The following are examples of such characteristics:

A batter who crouches at the plate ordinarily will have difficulty with high inside pitches, while a batter who stands up straight may not be able to hit the low pitch consistently.

A batter whose stride pulls him away from the plate usually has difficulty hitting a low pitch on the outside corner.

A batter who lunges or overstrides usually will have trouble with off-speed pitches like the curve or change of pace. Mixing up these pitches will keep him off stride. When throwing the fast ball, keep it high and inside.

A batter who steps in toward the plate on his stride often cannot hit consistently a fast ball high and inside.

A batter who is "nervous" at the plate, with a tendency to swing his bat back and forth repeatedly, is vulnerable to the waiting treatment. One who is particularly tense will grip the bat so tightly that his knuckle will be white. A catcher who spots this often will find a curve ball or change of pace effective.

Sizing up a specific hitter's weaknesses is an art in itself. The principles given will help the catcher to some degree, but experience will be the best teacher for both the pitcher and the catcher. The battery (catcher and pitcher) should take advantage of every opportunity to watch batters hit, even their own teammates.

Jim Turner, the great New York Yankee's pitching coach, once told the author that "When in doubt, throw the curve ball." This advice is good when the catcher has no other standard for judgment of a batter's weakness.

The Catcher and Pitcher Working Together: The catcher must know the characteristics of each of the pitchers he will catch. Every pitcher has a type of pitch upon which he relies and in which he has confidence. Whatever it may be, it is an important part of his equipment, since he believes in it. One of the first jobs the catcher must perform when practice begins is to learn the most effective pitch of each of the hurlers.

Many pitchers, when in a tight situation, will tend to rely heavily upon their favorite pitch. But when there are runners in scoring position and the batter has a known weakness, the catcher may prefer to pitch to that weakness instead of using the pitcher's favorite.

Confidence in each other is an important characteristic of an outstanding battery. If the catcher has experience and the pitcher is young, he should accept the signals given. There should be no great disagreement in calling pitches. There may be an occasion when the pitcher feels he can do a better job with a different pitch than the one which the catcher has called, and that should be his privilege.

The pitcher and the catcher should make every effort to understand each other. This is important to the relationship that should exist between the battery. The catcher is in the position of team leader, and most of the responsibility for a good working relationship is in his hands.

The Pitchout: The pitchout is a pitch thrown in such a way that it is impossbile for the batter to hit it. At the same time, it sets up the catcher to make a throw or gives him clearance to make a play at the plate, depending on the situation.

If the pitchout is called for a pick-off throw from the catcher to any base, it normally should be used only when there is an excellent chance of getting the runner. The game situation will determine if a pitchout should be called. Some coaches do not like for it to be used unless there are two outs. They believe with fewer than two outs, a wild throw will advance the runner, and his chance of scoring becomes greater, since more batters will have an opportunity to drive him in.

When the catcher's team is one or more runs ahead, the opposition is not likely to take chances. The logical play, therefore, is to get the hitter, since the runners will be playing safe. When the defense is a run or more behind, pick-offs should be attempted only if the catcher is sure he can get the runner. If he does not throw well, the pick-off should not be attempted, since a wild throw will give the opposing team an even greater margin.

The pitchout also is used when a player is intentionally put on base with a deliberate base on balls. In this situation the pitch should be kept outside, where the batter can not hit the ball without stepping on the plate. The catcher must stay in his box until the pitcher releases the ball. When an intentional pass is given right-handed batter, the catcher should stand as far right in the box as possible. As the pitch is released, he steps to the right to make the catch. The procedure is reversed on a left-handed batter.

POINTS TO REMEMBER

The following points are tips for catchers:
1. Provide a steady target, and catch the ball as close to the plate as possible.
2. Know the pitchers' strengths and weaknesses.
3. Call all plays in front of the plate.
4. Try to catch the latter part of a pitcher's pre-game warm-up.
5. Use a wider stance if the pitcher is wild.
6. Remember to control the speed at which the pitcher works.
7. Catch high pitches from above and bring them down.
8. Do not block the umpire's vision in catching high pitches.
9. Stay as close to the batter as possible with men on base.
10. Take only one step when throwing to a base unless it is a bad pitch.
11. Never make a random throw to a base.
12. Always put on a play with an infielder when signalling for a pitchout.
13. Make the throw to third base on the inside of the diamond.
14. Cover home correctly on throws from the outfield.
15. Remember the catcher must be a take-charge man and a real hustler.

16. Keep the body square to the diamond on low pitches.
17. Expect every pitch thrown to be a wild pitch.
18. Study each batter for weaknesses and catalogue them in the mind.
19. Check the defensive position of the infielders and outfielders frequently.
20. Wear catching equipment during infield practice, since it must be worn in the game.
21. Do not block home plate without possession of the ball.
22. Back up throws to first base with no one on base.
23. Remember that trouble in throwing may be attributed to feet movement and to the body being off balance.
24. Pick up bunts with two hands, scooping the ball into the mitt.
25. Bring the mitt up to the shoulder when throwing.

9

THE SCIENCE OF PITCHING

Experienced baseball coaches long have regarded pitching as responsible for from 50 to 75 percent of a team's chances of winning a single game. Of course, the percentage depends upon the age of the players and the class of baseball, amateur or professional.

Pitching is an art—the art of deception. The pitcher's job is to get the batter out, and this is done through a deception on his part. The batter must swing or take a called strike for each ball that passes through or even touches an area of about five cubic feet. The strike zone is more than a flat space area 17 inches wide extending vertically from the top of the batter's knees to the armpits. It also has depth. The pitcher throws at a three dimensional area slightly more than 217 square inches at the base, or knee-height, extending upward about 36 inches to the armpit, and forming a solid five space column of 7,812 cubic inches (Diag. 9-1). This space is the actual pitching target, and the pitcher must take advantage of every cubic inch of it. In teaching the fine art of pitching, the coach must understand the underlying principles and be able to communicate these to his pitchers.

Rotation of the baseball is a basic fundamental which each coach must understand because it is vital to outstanding pitching. The rotation or spin of the ball affects direction, and since every naturally thrown ball spins, the pitcher should know not only how it is spinning but to what degree the spin affects it.

Some coaches recommend painting two spots the size of a half-dollar on opposite sides of a regulation baseball. It must be kept clean, so they can be seen when it is in flight. Two pitchers standing about twenty feet apart throw the ball back and forth noting how it turns each time it leaves the hand. The pitcher should not worry about curve, speed, or control, but should make a mental note of how the the ball turns. He should experiment with different grips to see if he can obtain more rotation as he changes the finger pressures on the ball. The two fingers and the thumb in contact with the

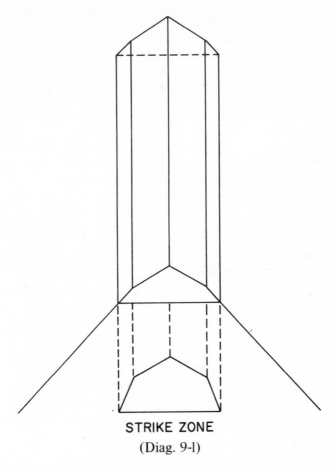

STRIKE ZONE

(Diag. 9-1)

baseball when it is gripped normally are the three pressure points which affect its rotation.

Greater speed is sometimes obtained by changing finger pressure. Velocity or speed is very important to the pitcher, and he should make every effort to find the best grip. Speed in pitching comes from the long whip-like action of the arm. It is increased by the spring of the elbow, the push off the mound, and the snap of the loose wrist. It is true that natural throwing speed is something with which each pitcher is born, but the coach can make suggestions that will enable him to get the most from his physical assets.

If it is true that pitching is approximately seventy-five percent of the difference between winning and losing, the wise coach will devote a major portion of his efforts toward improving his pitchers' abilities.

Qualifications of the Pitcher. The basic requirements for an aspiring pitcher are to have natural throwing ability and to be able to throw hard. There are exceptions to this requirement, but this is a basic toward being a successful pitcher. The various pitches such as the curve, or the change of pace can be learned. The pitcher must be in sound physical condition and stay that way, since playing his position requires considerable effort. He must possess strength, endurance, poise and determination. He must be intelligent enough to understand the complexities of game strategy, and he must be willing to work hard.

Most successful pitchers are men of strong physique, loose muscles, and frequently rangey. There are enough exceptions, however, to indicate that almost any kind of build will serve if a man wants to pitch and is willing to work. A small player with a good loose wrist who has coordination between arm and body can develop into an effective pitcher.

The Technique of Pitching. The proper form and delivery in pitching are different for each individual. Most pitchers throw the ball from a three-quarter overhand delivery, and this is the one usually taught the beginner, since it is the most natural for most players. But the coach must help the pitcher determine which is best for him, so he may reach his maximum potential. Any breaking pitches are more effective when delivered from the overhand or three-quarter position. It is not desirable to force a pitcher into the overhand pattern. A player who has been pitching with a natural sidearm or underhand delivery can sometimes make the change, but he should not unless after some practice he feels that the three-quarter or overhand action is natural and comfortable.

Only one type of delivery, regardless of the kind of pitch, should be used until the pitcher has completely mastered it. After he has perfected his natural motion, he may occasionally use a different type with considerable effectiveness, since the ball will be approaching the batter from a different angle. It should be remembered that if a pitcher uses more than one kind of delivery, he should not form the habit of throwing a specific type of pitch always in connection with the same delivery. In other words, he should be careful to avoid pitching a curve ball through one angle, and a fast ball habitually through another. It is desirable that he be able to throw all types of pitches from any type of delivery which he uses regularly.

Position on the Pitcher's Rubber. Every young pitcher should learn two positions on the pitcher's rubber: the windup position when no one is on base, and the set position with runners on base.

Wind-up Position: To assume the wind-up position, the pitcher places his pivot foot on the rubber, with the forward spikes over its front edge and the striding foot behind it. The gloved hand hangs loosely at his side, while the ball is held in the bare hand and hidden behind the body. The eyes are on the target (Fig. 9-1).

Fig. 9-1.

The delivery is started with a backward swing of the arms, and the upper half of the body is bent forward. The rear foot may slide backward slightly toward second base, and the knees are slightly bent but firm. Most of the weight of the body is now on the pivot foot.

The action is now reversed as the body is straightened, and the arms are swung forward and up to a position just above the forehead. The pitcher must be careful not to block his own view of the plate with either arm. As the arms are swung upward, the pivot foot is turned outward so its outside edge is resting against the inside edge of the rubber (Fig. 9-2). By placing the foot in this position, the pitcher is able to get a good balance, with a little more weight on the striding foot than on the pivot foot.

To get the maximum forward drive, the overhand pitcher should bring the knee of his free foot up high across the body as the arms

Fig. 9-2.

swing down and back. This leg action bends and pivots the body backward as the pitcher strides forward with the free foot, and the entire body goes into the pitch like an uncoiling spring, giving the maximum power and drive. At the time of the backward bend and pivot, the pitcher keeps his eyes on the target by looking over his front shoulders. The sidearm and underhand pitcher will not lift the free knee as high as the overhand pitcher but will use a more sideward pivot.

The stride foot should be pointing toward the plate with the hips and shoulders pivoting toward the batter. All of the body actions are forward, and the ball is released with a snap of the wrist.

When the stride foot comes forward, the pitcher should land on the balls of his feet, not on the heels. Many young pitchers think that the farther they stride the harder they will throw. This certainly is not true. If the pitcher is landing on his heels, he is overstriding, and this fault will affect his body balance and control. It should be remembered that the front leg should be bent slightly if the pitcher is to get on top of the ball. It is very difficult to bend the back if the front leg is stiff.

After the pitch is released, the pitching arm comes forward and down across the body in front of the striding knee. The pivot foot pushes off and swings to a position almost parallel or slightly ahead of the striding foot, so that the weight is well under control. Thus the pitcher is in a position to go in any direction (Fig. 9-3). If the ball is hit hard and directly at him, he can then protect himself as well as field the ball.

Fig. 9-3.

The motion the pitcher uses in delivering the ball should be the same regardless of the type of pitch to be made. This is important since many inexperienced pitchers often tip off the batter to what they will deliver by a slight change in action.

Set Position: The set position is used when the pitcher must hold runners on first base, first and second base, first and third base or all bases. Usually with the bases full, the pitcher will take the set-position only when he expects the squeeze or a steal of home.

To take the set position, a right-handed pitcher places the right foot in contact with the inside edge of the pitcher's rubber and the striding foot a comfortable distance ahead toward the plate (Fig. 9-4). When holding a runner on first base, the pitcher must keep

Fig. 9-4.

himself in a position to see the runner. This usually can be done by placing the front foot slightly toward first base. When holding a runner on second base, the foot is placed more in line with home plate (Fig. 9-5). Some pitchers keep the weight evenly distributed on both feet as they get the signs from the catcher. Others prefer to put more weight on the back foot. Whichever position is more natural for the pitcher should be used. It is important that the ball be hidden from the batter at this time (Fig. 9-6).

After receiving the sign, the pitcher should stretch both arms overhead, to loosen any binding of the uniform around the shoulders. Then he brings the arms down slowly to a comfortable position at the waist, where the hands are brought together, with the forearms parallel to the ground. The arms are relaxed against the

Fig. 9-5.

Fig. 9-6.

body with the ball in contact with the throwing hand and the glove (Fig. 9-7). The ball must come to rest in this position for one second before the pitch.

Fig. 9-7.

The pitcher must be careful not to fall into a pattern of looking at the runner the same number of times or taking the same amount of time between deliveries, or the baserunner who is alert will be able to get a good jump, if he desires to steal.

Usually the throw to first base is most effective as the pitcher is bringing his hands down to the set position. If the runner is taking his lead during this period, the pitcher will catch him leaning toward second base.

Some pitchers do not stretch at all when pitching from the set position. They simply bring both hands together at the waist, pausing one second before delivering the ball. This is excellent strategy when the pitcher thinks that the runner may try to steal on the pitch.

Whether the pitcher takes his stretch or not, he must remember that quickness is the key to picking men off base.

The lefthanded pitcher is in a better position to hold the runner on first base because he is facing in that direction when he takes his stretch. He can use the knee kick and still throw to first base or the plate. An excellent move to pick a runner off first base is for the pitcher to cock the knee, look toward first, and then toward the plate as he throws to first. (Fig. 9-8).

Fig. 9-8.

Sometimes the pitcher can throw to the plate without the knee kick if he is expecting a steal. This maneuver will often catch the runner flatfooted and unable to get the good jump.

THE BASIC PITCHES

There are three basic pitches which all pitchers should learn to throw: the fast ball, the curve, and the change of pace. In professional baseball other pitches are common, such as the slider and the knuckle ball, but they are not recommended for the young pitcher.

The Fast Ball. The most important pitch for the young pitcher to master is the fast ball. A fast ball does not mean overpowering speed, which is a gift. Many pitchers capable of throwing hard never seem to fool a batter with their quickness because the ball travels in a straight line. To master the fast ball, the pitcher must have control of it and the ability to make it move.

The grip is the first fundamental to be learned. The ball should be held so the fingers of the throwing hand make the best contact on the seams of the ball. The grip ordinarily will depend upon the individual pitcher, and he should experiment until he finds the one that is most efficient for him. Many pitchers hold the ball with the first two fingers on top and across the seams at their widest part (Fig. 9-9). The thumb is underneath and the third finger along the side of the ball. Other pitchers grip the ball with the first two fingers along the seams at their narrowest part.

Fig. 9-9.

Many pitching coaches have used a test to check the tightness of the fingers holding the baseball. The pitcher holds it in his pitching hand with the same grip he uses in the game. The coach flicks two fingers against it, trying to knock it from the pitcher's hand. If the grip is too tight, the pitcher will retain the baseball in his hand. If the coach knocks it from the pitcher's hand, he assumes the finger pressure is correct. If the baseball is gripped too hard or too deep in the hand, it will not sail or move. The baseball should be gripped firmly for the fast ball, but the wrist should not be locked. A pitcher who grips the ball too tightly may wear blisters on his finger tips.

Regardless of what grip the pitcher uses, he should continually work to produce the "hop" on his fast ball. This results from the release of the ball, which creates the rotation and determines the course taken by the pitch. The fast ball is released off the ends of the first and second fingers, and since the second finger is longer, it will leave that finger last. Many pitchers have a natural "hop" or movement on their fast ball, and those who do not should practice releasing the pitch from the tip of the second finger on the side toward the third finger. Slightly greater pressure exerted by the second finger as the ball is released gives it the rotation that makes it hop. A definite wrist snap should be used as it is released. At Lipscomb the pitching staff has had success in making the fast ball move by following through with the hand and wrist snap toward the glove hand rather than toward the ground.

The good straight overhand fast ball has a tendency to rise because of the upward rotation of the ball on the release. The fast ball delivered from a three-quarter overhand delivery tends to rise slightly and move to the right of a right-handed pitcher.

The sidearm delivery is similar in that the ball will move toward the right, if delivered by a righthanded pitcher. The rotation of the ball is sideward in the direction of release. The effectiveness of the side-armer is enhanced if the batter places his weight on his heels and leans away from the pitch. It is important that the pitch be thrown on the outside half of home plate. If it is inside, the batter has a chance to hit it, even though he is leaning away from it. This pitch generally should be kept low.

At Lipscomb the pitching staff is instructed to throw two different speeds of fast balls, called the 90% and 98% fast balls. The regular fast ball is the 90% and the extra fast is the 98%, which will have something extra on it, but the pitcher will still have balance and body control. In the 100% fast ball this may be lost. The outstanding pitcher usually possesses two different speed fast balls.

The Curve Ball. The initial grip and arm action for throwing the curve ball should be identical with that of a fast ball, so the pitcher does not give away the pitch before it is delivered. As the windup is started and the ball lifted over the head, the fingers slide parallel to the seam, so the second finger has good contact along a seam. It usually is gripped more tightly with the second finger, while the index finger merely acts as a guide.

Some pitchers shift their middle and index fingers until the middle finger is on the curved part of the seam (Fig. 9-10). Others

Fig. 9-10.

turn the hand from the back of the ball to the outside so the curved part of the seam is inside the hand and then place the middle finger along the seam. The middle and index fingers are close together, and the thumb is flat on the ball (Fig. 9-11).

As the pitching arm is brought forward and the ball is about to be released, the wrist is snapped inward. This snapping of the wrist is very important, since it causes the ball to spin faster and the curve to break sharply. The wrist must be relaxed for the pitcher to get the

Fig. 9-11.

proper wrist snap and to utilize the entire length of his fingers. There is a downward pull as the ball comes off the surface of the middle finger and rolls over the index finger. The pitcher should be striving for all possible downward rotation on the curve, since this is what makes the ball hard to hit. A shortened stride helps the pitcher to get more break on the ball since it is easier for the arm to follow through in a downward direction. The pitcher should feel that his hand has inscribed a circle beginning where the throwing arm started forward and ending at his opposite knee.

A recommended way to get the "feel" of the curve ball spin is to hold the ball without the thumb on it, jamming it back into hand and snapping the wrist as it is released. At first the ball should be thrown only a few feet. As the pitcher gets the "feel" of the spin, he may lay his thumb back on the ball and become accustomed to longer throws, working with the catcher. The coach should check the spin of the ball by standing directly behind the catcher. A ball that is spinning fast and about a single axis will show a small dot on its upper side. This spot is the axis around which the ball is spinning. If it is not spinning correctly, an oblong spot will show.

The pitcher should not try to throw the curve ball with a crook in his arm. It should be almost extended as it is during a fast ball pitch.

An effective curve ball must be thrown accurately, and this can be accomplished only through concentrated practice. The pitcher must concentrate on the spot from which the ball will start to break and on the amount of its curve. To be of any value, the curve ball must be thrown below the batter's belt. High curve balls do not break as sharply as do low curve balls. The curve ball thrown high permits the batter to see the spin and judge its final break while in flight. The good breaking curve ball which can be thrown over the plate for a strike will make a pitcher a top winner.

Several common causes for the hanging curve ball will be discussed here. Usually the pitcher who is throwing the curve ball in the batter's eyes is *not pulling down hard on the ball* as he comes forward with the wrist. He should try to bring the shoulder of his throwing arm down as he releases the ball. Young pitchers have trouble *getting on top of the ball* to keep it from hanging. As mentioned earlier, the pitcher must shorten the stride to do this. It is impossible to get on top of the ball if the stride is too long. Pitchers who have trouble *bending the back* usually have trouble with the curve hanging. Other points which the coach must look for when the curve is hanging are poor *wrist action, releasing the ball too soon, gripping the ball too tightly, and gripping the ball too far back in the palm of the hand.*

The pitcher must remember that a wind blowing in from center-field may cause the curve to hang or fail to break properly. A wind blowing across the plate may keep the ball from breaking sharply. Also the curve will usually break faster in damp weather than in dry air.

The pitcher must concentrate on a low target at all times. He must concentrate, also, on bending his back and getting on top of the ball if he expects to throw the sharp curve. The excellent curve ball is a strike out pitch if thrown below the belt. It should be kept in mind that the down-breaking curve ball is a good pitch to force the batter to hit into a double play.

The Change of Pace. The change of pace is delivered with the same body and arm action as the fast ball, but it travels more slowly. In throwing the change of pace, some pitchers grip the ball as they normally do for their fast ball, but they jam the ball farther back into the thumb and index finger, taking the fingertips off the ball as it is released (Fig. 9-12). The ball is pushed forward off the middle

Fig. 9-12.

joints of the two fingers. To slow the ball more, the pitcher should "pull" the hand down, like pulling down a window shade.

This pitch can be thrown also by another method in which the ball is gripped loosely, well back in the palm of the hand, and then delivered with very litte pressure by the fingers. Usually three fingers are placed on top of the ball when this method is used (Fig. 9-13).

A slow curve may be pitched by holding the ball very loosely and then, on release, permitting it to roll over the second joint of the first finger, as in the ordinary curve ball. The fingertips should not touch the ball, and the looser the grip, the slower the pitch.

Many young pitchers like to throw the "slow curve" as a change-up pitch which is all right if thrown at the correct speed and to the right type of batter. The pitcher should never throw a change-up to a weak hitter but should overpower him with his best pitches. The speed of the pitch must deceive the hitter, or it will be easily judged, and he will fatten his batting average. This means the

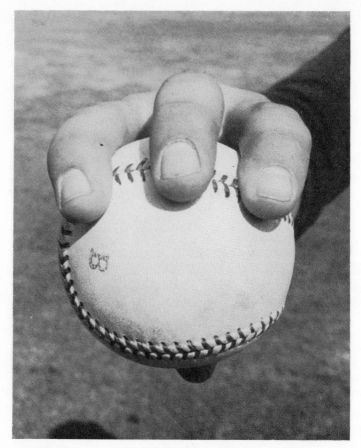

Fig. 9-13.

pitcher must work constantly to improve his control of the pitch and develop the correct speed to go along with his other pitches.

The young pitcher should not try to throw two or three change-up pitches, since it is difficult to control a great variety of finger grips. The pitcher must remember there must be a reason to utilize the pitch.

The Slider. The slider can be used successfully to keep the hitter off balance. It is usually easier to control than the curve ball because it does not break as much. To the batter it looks like a fast ball, but then at the last moment it breaks away from the righthanded hitter. A good fast ball pitcher can usually use the slider as his percentage pitch. It should be kept low and away to be effective, the exception being, perhaps, if the pitcher is attempting to jam an opposite side hitter.

The slider is pitched from an overhand delivery and thrown harder than the curve ball. It resembles the action needed to make a football spiral. It is held with the first finger placed on the outer seam at its narrowest part, the thumb contacting a seam underneath. To make it break in the same direction as the curve ball, it is delivered with a fairly stiff wrist, leaving the tip of the first finger on the thumb side. At the time of release, the wrist is slightly turned in, as though the pitcher were turning a door knob. This action causes the ball to rotate upward and slightly in the opposite direction of the side from which it is delivered.

Pitchers who normally throw with a stiff wrist can develop a slider easily. But for most pitchers, particularly the beginner, it will require a great deal of practice.

SPECIALTY PITCHES

The pitcher should not add a specialty pitch without carefully analyzing his strengths and weaknesses. There must be a reason for adding the pitch. First of all, the curve ball is needed along with the fast ball to force the batter to deal with pitches breaking on different planes. By changing speeds on both the curve and the fast ball, the pitcher forces the batter to contend not only with the different planes but also with the different speeds. The pitcher who possesses a fast ball, a curve, and a change of pace has quite a repertory of weapons with which to confuse the batter. If he can get these pitches over the plate, he need not spend his time trying to develop a freak pitch.

The Knuckle Ball. Of all the specialty pitches the knuckle ball is possibly the most famous. This type of pitch probably takes the most erratic course to the plate of any thrown. It may sink, curve to either side, or jump. Its movements are highly unpredictable. These qualities make it a very difficult pitch to control. The knuckle ball rotates very little and seems to explode one way or another as it approaches the plate.

Both the overhand and the sidearm pitcher may throw the knuckle ball. As in all breaking pitches, the irregular course of the ball is caused by air pressure, and the pitch is more effective when thrown into the wind or with a cross wind.

There are several methods of throwing this pitch. It can be thrown by digging the fingernails into the seams or by placing the first joints of one, two, or three fingers on the ball. Most professional pitchers who use this pitch throw the two finger knuckle ball. It is thrown with a dead wrist similar to the change-of-pace, but harder. This pitch is not recommended for young pitchers.

The Fork Ball. The fork ball is another pitch associated with pitchers of considerable experience, and the young pitcher should not attempt to master it. It can be thrown with either an overhand or sidearm delivery. The first and second fingers are spread wide, and the ball is held between them. They should not touch the seams, since the ball must slide from between them. The thumb is held underneath the ball touching the seam. There should be a vigorous wrist snap in delivery. The fork ball usually breaks in the same direction as a curve, but with little rotation, the pitch is not predictable. Since it is normally thrown at reduced speed, it can be used effectively as a change of pace if properly developed.

The Screw Ball. The screw ball is held the same as a fast ball, but the actual delivery is different. The screw ball action is an unnatural movement, because the back of the hand is turned inward, toward the body, as the arm starts forward to deliver the ball. At release, the thumb pushes the ball outward as pressure is exerted by the second finger, and it leaves the hand between the second and third fingers. On delivery, the back of the hand is turned to the batter, and the arm and wrist are rolled inward toward the body. The ball may be held tightly or loosely. If held loosely, the pitch will have the speed of a change-up. A good screw ball pitch will break in the opposite direction from a curve ball because its rotation is sideward. It is a pitch that is hard on the arm and should not be used by young players because of the unnatural arm action.

TYPES OF PITCHERS

Most pitchers may be classified in terms of their favorite and most effective pitches. Each type of pitcher approaches the game from different points of view, and this tends to classify them.

The fast ball pitcher is the one who depends primarily upon his speed in throwing the ball past the batter. The sandlot pitcher who strikes out a dozen men a game generally does it with a fast ball. In college baseball, such a pitcher would be more effective if he developed a change of pace and a fair curve. All of these pitches would require control, but the chief effectiveness lies in the difference in speed.

The curve ball pitcher ordinarily has a strong hand and a flexible wrist. The key to his success is to put spin on the ball. Curve balls should be kept low; so this type of pitcher must possess better control than a fast ball pitcher. Unless he happens to have a good fast ball, the curve ball pitcher will tend to use the fast one to set the batter up. This means the fast ball will be thrown on the corner of the plate, usually low and away from the hitter.

The control pitcher is more difficult to define, but he is thought of as one who pitches to the exact spot. If his control is sufficiently sharp and he has knowledge of hitter weaknesses, he often can get by with very little "stuff". This type of pitcher does not try to strike out the batter, but he makes careful use of various speeds and techniques in delivery to keep the hitter off balance.

DEVELOPMENT OF CONTROL

It is very difficult to be a successful pitcher without control. Most pitching authorities regard control as the most important feature of pitching. Control means the ability to throw the ball to a chosen target, even if it is outside the strike zone.

The three main essentials in acquiring control are a smooth delivery, constant practice, and concentration. Though giving adequate time to practice is a simple matter, most young pitchers never learn to concentrate during this period. Excellent control without total concentration in practice is very difficult. The pitcher should have a mental picture of the course he wants the ball to follow before he starts his initial move, and he must keep his eyes on the target throughout delivery. Though it is a simple matter for him to watch the target throughout the wind-up and delivery, he often will lapse into a habit of dropping his eyes momentarily from it. The pitcher must force himself to "bear down" and to concentrate on the catcher's mitt. He should never be guilty of "going to sleep" on the pitcher's mound. He must work hard at all times. Too many pitchers try to pace themselves to finish the entire ball game and as a result lose the game in the early innings.

Poor control usually results from some "flaw" in the delivery, which can be corrected. For the coach to aid the wild pitcher, he must recognize the basic causes of wildness, which are listed here:

Landing on the Heel: When the pitcher strides forward, he should not land on his heel. This jars the whole body and affects his control. The stride should be made on the ball of the foot.

Aiming the Ball: This is a very common cause of poor control, especially the momentary loss of control. This usually happens in a tight situation when the pressure is great. The pitcher should not let-up on a pitch to throw to a certain spot. He must believe he can get the batter out by using his best "stuff" and not aim the ball.

Taking Eyes off Target: Keeping the eyes steadily on the target has just been mentioned as an important trait in excellent control.

Throwing across the Body: When a pitcher throws across his body, he locks his hips and impedes smooth delivery. The pitcher should open his hips by striding more to the left, if a righthanded pitcher. To stride too far to the left, however, will dissipate his power. For further explanation, check Chapter 2 and Figure 2-2.

Physical Tiredness: The pitcher who is in poor physical condition will weaken in his control before the game is completed. Pitching rhythm is usually affected if he becomes tired, and his control will suffer. The pitcher will have enough problems on the mound without being wild because he is not in top physical shape. The pitcher's legs are very important to him in terms of conditioning, along with the basic stamina necessary to pitch a nine inning ball game.

Improper Body Balance: The pitcher who is off-balance during the wind-up will experience control problems. Learning to pivot and balance is vital to good control. The pitcher who can pivot and balance usually has excellent body and hip coordination. The pivot leg should be bent slightly at the knee to support the body weight as the hips are turned. The stiff leg will make it difficult to support the body weight.

Excessive Motion: The pitcher who puts too much effort into the wind-up will hinder his control. He must work to develop a smooth delivery. The no-wind-up delivery has helped several professional pitchers overcome this problem. The no-wind-up approach is recommended if the pitcher who has an exaggerated wind-up is wild. This is done by having the pitcher hold the ball in the glove in front of the belt buckle and then deliver it.

Different Arm Angle: Some pitchers use a different arm angle for every pitch. Such procedure makes it very difficult to learn a groove. For the young pitcher, it is important to throw every pitch from the same angle. If this is done, there is a better chance for him to have control.

A pitcher's position on the rubber may affect his control, even though he does not realize it. The pitcher should become accustomed to throwing from the same spot on the rubber on each pitch, and he should not move unless it is absolutely necessary. If he is throwing inside or outside of the strike zone and he cannot make other adjustments to get the ball over the plate, then he should move his pivot foot. If he consistently pitches toward the third base side of home plate, he should move his pivot foot toward the first base side of the rubber. If he consistently pitches toward the first base side, he should move his pivot foot toward the third base side of the rubber.

If the pitcher is consistently high, a slightly shorter stride in delivery will bring the ball down, and if his pitches are low, lengthening the stride will bring the ball up. At the same time, the catcher should attempt to give a better target to help him. No pitcher should ever try to match the opposing pitcher's stride on the mound. This may happen if the mound is not well-attended, and a hole is dug where the stride foot lands. Another pitcher may have a longer stride, and it would be a mistake to try to pitch from his "landing spot."

HOLDING A RUNNER ON BASE

Runner on First. Usually, the pitcher makes a throw to first base when the runner has too long a lead, or when a steal is expected. Sometimes such a throw will pick-off the runner. It will at least keep him close to the base. Many inexperienced pitchers do not throw to first base often enough. If a throw is made and the runner has to slide to get back, another throw should be made immediately.

In working from the set position, many pitchers throwing to first base make a different initial move from that used in delivering to the plate. This action often tips off a base runner. An example of this is the right-handed pitcher who makes an initial move with his shoulders, arms, body, legs or feet before pitching to the batter but lifts the right heel as the initial move to throw to first base. The baserunner by watching the right heel will know when the throwing is coming to first.

If the pitcher has a fault, he should develop and use the same initial move for the throw to first base and the delivery to the batter. This move should be light and natural, and so coordinated with the throw to first that it cannot be called a balk.

Some pitchers have a tendency to turn their left shoulders outward toward first base beyond the distance necessary for a proper stretch. The more the left shoulder faces first base, the greater the time needed to move it into the correct delivery position. The longer the time needed to deliver the ball to home plate, the greater the "jump" for the base runner stealing second base. The correct technique here is for the pitcher to move his eyes to see the base runner but not his shoulders. This also is a more effective way of seeing the target at home plate. The eyes can be moved very quickly and will not interfere with the body movement.

Unless a pitcher has been taught otherwise, he will tend to work in a definite rhythm, so much so that it can be reduced to a regular cadence count, one-two-three-four. If an alert base runner gets this count and starts his break just before the ball is delivered to the plate, he will have an excellent jump toward second base. The pitcher must vary the count in his delivery to the plate and on his throws to first base.

Many base runners develop a careless habit of which an alert pitcher can take advantage. When forced back to the base by a throw, some runners will lead off again as soon as the first baseman returns the ball to the pitcher. This kind of runner can sometimes be caught by a quick return throw just after receiving the ball.

If the base runner uses a crossover step in taking his lead, the pitcher can sometimes pick him off. The pitcher should time his throw to arrive just as the left foot crosses in front of the right. This places the runner in the position of taking another step with his right foot before he can recover and return to the base.

When the pitcher takes the set position and does not wish to deliver the baseball to home plate, he must remove his pivot foot from the front edge of the rubber to a position beyond the back edge of it. The pivot foot must be lifted clear of the rubber and placed in the ground behind its second base side. This must be done before the pitcher breaks his hands, to avoid committing a balk. This same procedure is used when he wishes to put the ball in play, such as on an appeal play.

When the pitcher takes the set position and the runner starts for second base, he should step off the rubber as just described and make his turn directly toward the runner. If the runner stops, the pitcher should immediately run directly toward him, making him commit himself toward a base. As the pitcher charges off the mound, the second baseman should run forward on the baseline ready to take a short throw. If the runner breaks toward first and the pitcher throws to that base, he should immediately back up first base on the rundown until someone else can take his position.

Runner on Second. When there is a runner on second base, the pitcher assumes the set position before the delivery to home plate. From the set position, in a throw to second base, he should make the long turn—a righthanded pitcher turning left, and a lefthanded pitcher turning right. The base runner is more likely to assume that the pitch is going to the plate than if a short turn is made. In throwing to second base, it is necessary to step in that direction, but the pitcher may, however, turn and make a feint to throw.

Some pitchers cannot learn to make the long turn effectively. If they cannot, they should use the short turn, which means the righthanded pitcher turns right and a lefthanded pitcher turns left. If at any time the runner starts for third base and stops, the pitcher should step off the rubber and run directly at him.

When both second and third bases are occupied, and the runner on second starts for third, the pitcher should immediately step off the rubber and run directly toward the runner who left second base. The pitcher should then force the runner to third. If the runner on third base breaks for home, he should be played.

Runner on Third. When there is a runner on third base and the score is close, the squeeze play or the steal of home are a possibility. The pitcher is the most important individual in breaking up a squeeze or steal. When a righthanded batter is at bat and the base runner makes a break for home plate, the pitcher should make his pitch at the hips of the batter. By using this type of pitch, the batter is driven away from the plate, and the catcher is in good position to tag the runner. This is also a very difficult pitch to bunt.

If the squeeze play is on with a lefthanded hitter at bat, the pitch should be low and outside. This pitch is difficult to bunt and places the catcher in good position to make the tag on the runner.

The catcher and the pitcher should understand that regardless of the pitch which may have been called, when the squeeze or steal is on, it automatically is changed to a fast ball unless there are two strikes on the batter. Then the pitch should remain the same and be thrown for a strike. The runner will have to slow down, since the batter must swing at the ball or be called out. If he does not swing, the catcher has a little more time and is in good position to tag the incoming runner. A change of pace should not be called if there is a possibility of a squeeze play or a steal of home.

THE PITCHERS' WARM UP

One of the most important responsibilities of the pitcher is to warm up properly before the game. During this period, he not only must bring his body efficiency to its highest peak, but also must get himself ready mentally for the job ahead of him. Each pitcher must work out his own warm-up procedure, since he not only has to be ready to pitch but also must believe that he is ready.

The length of time for the warm-up depends upon the individual and the weather conditions. On a warm day, the muscles respond more quickly than on a cold one, when more pitches are required to do the job. Before a pitcher goes to the field on a cold day, his throwing muscles can be loosened by a light massage with a rubbing balm. For added warmth and protection, he should wear a wool sweat shirt.

The pitcher should not throw a ball at all until he is ready to warm up. He should start with a few close pitches and gradually move back to regulation distance. The first pitches should be easy, straight balls, with a gradual increase in speed. He should not throw hard or try any breaking pitches until he begins to sweat. Adherence to this rule will prevent injury to the pitching arm. When the pitcher feels he is ready to throw other types of pitches which will be used in the game, he again should throw easily at first and gradually increase the tempo. As this change is made from one pitch to another, the catcher should be informed.

After the first few pitches, the catcher should set his mitt as a target, about waist high and over the plate. As the warm-up progresses and other types of pitches are thrown, the target should be changed to high and low, and over the inside and outside corners of the plate. The warm-up should be completed with several breaking balls followed by four or five fast balls delivered at top speed.

Many young pitchers do not throw enough pitches from the set position during warm-up. As a result, they often lose their control in the game when they must work with men on base. After the pitcher has properly warmed-up, he should throw at least one-half of his pitches from the set position.

When the weather is hot, the warm-up period should be timed so that the pitcher will have a few minutes to rest before the game starts. On cool days he may prefer not to rest after the warm-up, to eliminate any possibility of cooling off. Cold weather forces him to wear a jacket at all times, except when he is throwing.

The coach should keep a careful eye on his players' throwing, especially the pitching staff. Many young players are not capable of following their own judgment in warming up. They often will throw too hard too soon and too long, and develop sore arms. Warming up is an important phase of the game of baseball which cannot be overemphasized to the players.

RELIEF PITCHER'S WARM-UP

An outstanding relief pitcher is a valuable asset to any team and may win more ball games than the starters. Some teams have squad members for this particular duty, but others frequently are forced to use regular starters on their off days. So far as the actual game situation is concerned, the relief pitcher's preparation does not differ from the starter's. If he is the long relief pitcher, he should warm up sufficiently as the game starts so he can be ready with only eight or ten pitches. Whenever the game situation indicates that he is likely to be called, he immediately should start to warm-up again. This may happen several times during a game and is one of the real problems which face relief pitchers. It is a touchy assignment to get ready quickly to the point of greatest pitching efficiency after a half-dozen false starts. If the reliever must pitch from the set position when he goes into the game, he should pitch from it in the warm up.

When the relief pitcher approaches the mound, he should have all the necessary information concerning the game situation.

THE FIFTH INFIELDER

The moment the pitcher releases the ball to the batter, he becomes the fifth infielder. His ability to handle batted balls and to diagnose play situations is sometimes the difference between winning or losing. In the course of a game, he may be required to handle batted balls, cover a base, make throws to a base, and back up plays.

His failure to perform any of these duties properly may cost the team the victory. The pitcher is not only the fifth infielder—he must be an efficient one.

As the ball is delivered, the pitcher brings himself into his fielding position, as described previously. If there are no runners on base and a ground ball is hit hard and directly at him, he should move off the mound after fielding the ball. This places him in better position to throw and gives the first baseman time to cover the base. The throw should never be lobbed but should be thrown with reasonable speed as soon as the first baseman reaches the base.

The pitcher should remember that on slow ground balls it is almost impossible to make a play at second or third base on an advancing runner. A good rule for most pitchers to follow is always throw to first base any time they are pulled off the mound in fielding a ground ball, unless the catcher calls for a throw to another base.

If a ground ball is fielded by the pitcher and a base runner who has made a break stops between bases, the pitcher should play him by advancing to a point slightly ahead of him. If the pitcher can tag the runner, he should do so.

FIELDING BUNTS AND THROWING TO BASES

If the right-handed pitcher fields a ball bunted close to the third base line and the throw is to first, he should move quickly to a position directly in front of the ball. The right leg is braced as he stops and sets to throw in one step.

The left-handed pitcher usually fields a bunted ball close to the first base line in front of his left foot and pivots to his right to make the throw. In many cases the pitcher's back will be toward first base as he fields a ball bunted along the third base line, and he should pivot again to the right to make the throw.

The pitcher must be careful in fielding bunts or slow rollers, since often the spin on the ball makes it hard to handle. If it is fumbled, the throw should go automatically to first base. If the ball is fielded close to the first base line, the throw should be made on the inside of first base.

The pitcher must use good judgment on a bunt which rolls down the foul line and make the decision whether to field it or let it roll. If it does roll foul, slap it with the bare or gloved hand, so it will be dead.

When the pitcher fields a ground ball on which a play can be made at second base and the shortstop is covering, the throw should be a few feet to the third base side and chest high. If the second baseman covers, the throw should be a few feet toward first base side of second. If either infielder reaches the base before the throw starts, it should be directly to the base.

The speed with which a pitch is thrown to a base is dependent primarily on the distance. Long throws should be hard, while shorter throws can be reduced in speed to make them easier to handle. Except under unusual conditions, the lob throw should not be used. It is often inaccurate under pressure, and the change in speed sometimes confuses the player who has to catch it.

The general procedure in fielding ground balls is for the pitcher to make the shortest possible pivot in throwing to bases.

COVERING THE BASES

Covering First Base. When a ground ball is hit to the left of the pitcher and he cannot field it, he should immediately move to cover first base. He should stop only if it goes through the infield or the first baseman is able to cover the base. If the first baseman can make the play himself, he should wave the pitcher off. The key to this play is for the pitcher to get off the mound quickly. It is surprising how often pitchers fail to react to a ball hit to their left. In executing this play, the pitcher should run to a spot about fifteen feet from first base and foul line. Then he should proceed inside the line and parallel to it (Fig. 9-14). He should not watch the fielder at all until

Fig. 9-14.

he has located the base. If he looks toward the infield too soon, he most likely will be thrown off stride and miss the base or will be forced into an awkward position to make the catch. It is important that the pitcher receives the ball a few steps before reaching the base if possible, so he will have time to look down and make sure he touches it. If he reaches first base before the throw can be made, he should stop, placing his right foot on the inside edge of the base, and stretch out for the throw. The toss to the pitcher should be made about shoulder high and to the glove hand side. After tagging it, he should stop quickly and turn back toward the infield if other runners are on base.

Pitchers should be taught to take nothing for granted, as the first baseman may go for a ball beyond his reach, thereby leaving the base uncovered. The pitcher must then take the throw from the second baseman.

If the ball is fielded by the first baseman and the throw goes to second base, the pitcher should run directly to first base, placing his right foot on its inside edge, and then stretch out for the throw. If a bunt or slow roller get past the pitcher, he again should run directly to the base, making the stretch if possible. If there is not enough time, he should take the throw on the run.

Covering Second Base. If the second baseman and the shortstop both go into the outfield for a short fly ball leaving second base uncovered, the pitcher should cover. If the third or first baseman covers that base, the pitcher takes the one which is left open.

Covering Third Base. When a runner is on second base and both the shortstop and third baseman go back after a fly ball, the pitcher should cover third base.

If first base is occupied and a bunt or a slow ground ball is hit along the third base line which the third baseman fields, the pitcher should cover third if the third baseman cannot get back to the base and the shortstop or the catcher fails to cover. If the catcher covers third, the pitcher should cover home plate.

Covering Home Plate. When runners are in scoring position, on second or third base, and a ball gets away from the catcher, the pitcher should cover home plate. He also covers it when third base is occupied, there are fewer than two outs, and the catcher leaves his position in an attempt to catch a foul fly ball. If he fails to cover in this situation, the runner on third may easily score after the ball is caught.

In taking a throw from the catcher for a play on a runner coming into the plate, the pitcher should take a position in fair territory just in front of the plate and facing the catcher. If the throw is accurate, the pitcher will ordinarily make his turn to the right to tag the runner. Should the throw be wide, he should dive for the third base side of home plate after catching the ball, if there is a play on the runner.

PITCHING ROTATION

One of the primary responsibilities of a coach is to decide who will pitch a particular game. This decision will be made according to the dictates of the schedule. The more frequently a team plays, the more important the pitching rotation. Therefore, the professional manager is more concerned than the college, high school, or little league coach. When championships are determined by one or two games, the coach must approach every game as a crucial one. This means he must put his best pitcher against the most formidable opponent. In college and high school, he usually pitches the "ace" as often as he is ready physically to throw. It might be noted here that the coach has a responsibility to his players not to use them when they have not had adequate rest.

When rotation is being taken into consideration, the coach might do well to analyze the following:

1. the type of hitter on a particular team. Use a curve ball pitcher if the opposing team likes the fast ball.
2. the type of pitcher—whether he throws left or righthanded.
3. the success that a given pitcher has had against a specific team.
4. the effectiveness of a certain type of pitcher in a particular ball park. (Fast ball pitchers do better in large ball parks.)
5. the weather conditions.

There are certain peculiarities a coach must consider when planning his pitching rotation. Some pitchers seem more effective in crucial games against strong teams. Other pitchers do better at night, in warm weather, or on cool days. At Lipscomb, there have been pitchers who were stronger on the road than in their own ball park. Some pitchers are slow starters and do not hit their stride until mid-season, while others start strong and tail-off toward the end of the season. Others have the ability to beat one particular team consistently, while finding it difficult to beat other teams. The coach must pick the right man for the right situation as often as possible.

POINTS TO REMEMBER

The following are points on the fine art of pitching which each pitcher would do well to remember:

1. Always keep the eyes on the target.

2. Do not rush the stride or overstride.
3. Keep the ball in the glove until the last moment.
4. Open up and rotate the hips.
5. Be quick with the top part of the body.
6. Whip the arm through—speed it up.
7. Snap the wrist with strong hand action.
8. Wear a large glove that will help to cover up the pitches.
9. Swing the glove hand toward the hitter.
10. Follow through and try to keep the feet parallel.
11. Try to stay ahead of the hitter at all times.
12. On the day before a game, warm up lightly and get plenty of rest.
13. Wild high constantly means one of the following: overstriding, turning the ball loose too soon, or not bending the back.
14. Never pitch from the top of the pitching rubber.
15. Use as little leg action as possible with men on base.
16. Do not try to throw the curve ball too hard.
17. Never deliver the ball to the plate when an infielder is out of fielding position.
18. Always cover first base on any ball hit to the left of the mound.
19. If a runner is caught off first base, always back up this base until another player takes the position.
20. Always know where the infielders and outfielders are playing.
21. Always assume the responsibility of covering any base left open.
22. Take the sign with pivot foot in contact with the rubber.
23. Practice looking a runner back at third base during the wind-up.
24. Always be sure that spikes are in good condition.
25. Back off the rubber when in stretch position, if the runner at first base disappears.

10

FIRST THINGS FIRST

There is a saying in baseball that "anyone can play first." Few coaches ever question it. However, the truth is that the first baseman is one of the most important men on the field because he gets more chances than anyone else except the catcher. The first baseman may not be the most efficient fielder in the infield, but he must have quick hands and be able to handle all kinds of thrown balls.

Experts also contend that a left-handed first baseman has a great advantage over a right-hander. On throws to second or third base, he *does* have an advantage. He merely has to step in the direction of the throw as he makes the catch, while the right-hander must turn his body. But this advantage is so *slight* that it is almost meaningless.

Size is a definite asset. A tall man can reach farther and give the other fielders a better target. This does not mean that the tallest boy should automatically be installed at first. A smaller player can compensate for his lack of height with speed and quickness.

Though a good arm is desirable, it need not be as strong as the other arms in the infield. Excellent footwork is particularly important for handling bad throws and shifting properly. Also essential is the ability to size up situations and to make the basic throws effectively. All these techniques can be mastered through hard and constant practice.

The other players must have complete confidence in the first baseman's ability to handle all balls thrown at him. Otherwise they may become too cautious and begin aiming their throws.

Receiving Throws. On a play to first, the first baseman runs directly to the base as soon as the ball is hit. Since he must get there in time to be in position, he must not play so far from the base that it will take an extra effort to be there before the throw.

Upon reaching the base, he uses various techniques. His first responsibility is to find the base and maintain complete body balance. Usually a first baseman locates the base with his heel, then faces the thrower, placing his feet a few inches in front of the base, approximately base-width apart.

To achieve the maximum stretch, he must line up his body directly with the thrower. *He should not shift until the throw is on the way.* This is a split-second move that is fundamental to good defensive play. A young player frequently errs by placing one foot on the base and reaching before the fielder releases the ball. This position ties him up and prevents his shifting.

The first baseman should learn all he possibly can about the other infielders. He should know, for instance, if a fielder has a strong or a weak arm, and whether his throws take off or sink.

When receiving a throw from his right, the right-handed first baseman places his left foot against the outfield side of the base, and then steps with his right foot toward the throw for the catch (Fig. 10-1). However, some professionals prefer crossing over with the

Fig. 10-1.

left foot and backhanding the ball. On a wild throw, the main objective is to stop the ball and then if possible to tag the base.

On a throw to his left, the first baseman places his right foot against the inside corner of the base and steps toward the throw with his left foot (Fig. 10–2). If the throw is wide, he leaves the bag for the catch, then tags the runner coming down the line—making sure not to interfere with him.

Fig. 10-2.

When the ball is thrown directly at him, the right-handed first baseman places his right foot on the second-base side of the base and faces the thrower (Fig. 10-3). The reverse is true for the left-handed first baseman. On a close play he must stretch as far as possible in order to make the catch as quickly as possible. The long stretch often spells the difference between an "out" or "safe" call.

As soon as he catches the ball, he should pull his contact foot off the base. On throws received below his waist, the *palm* of his glove points upward (Fig. 10-3). On throws above his waist, the *fingers* of his glove point upward as shown in Figure 10-2.

Throws in the dirt should be fielded as close as possible to the point of contact. If the baseman cannot take the throw on the short hop, he should try to block it with his body. Some throws can be

Fig. 10-3.

taken on the long hop. The art of stopping the low throw can be improved through constant practice.

On high throws directly over the bag, the baseman may have to leap straight up to make the catch. He should try to come down on the infield side of the base on such plays. If the throw is beyond his reach, he will have to leave the bag and then try for the out.

On a throw from the home-plate area, the first baseman places his left foot on the second-base side of the base and extends his glove toward the thrower as a target (Fig. 10-4).

On a throw to the foul-line side of first, the baseman steps across the base into foul territory with his left foot and places his right (contact) foot on the foul-line side of the base (Fig. 10-5). As soon as he makes the catch, he pivots towards the infield for a possible play elsewhere.

Fielding Grounders. The first baseman's deployment is dictated by his fielding ability and the game situation. He must know the hitters in order to play them properly, and he must also be aware of

Fig. 10-4.

Fig. 10-5.

the score, outs, inning, count, and the ability of the baserunners.

He must consider also both his and the second baseman's ground-covering ability, and know how the second baseman deploys for the various hitters. This will enable him to decide how far to play from the base. *Note:* The second baseman should always call for any grounder between himself and the first baseman which he believes he can handle.

Since aggressiveness is a great asset to any infielder, the first baseman must defy the ball, as it were. He must learn to charge the ball quickly, whenever possible, and to field it on a favorable bounce. If this is impossible, he must learn to short-hop it.

Since the ball does not always take a true bounce, the first baseman must carry his hands below the expected height of the bounce, as he can raise his hands quicker than he can lower them. It is also important that he does not pull his hands away from the ball too quickly, since this tendency produces many unnecessary errors.

The first baseman has a decided advantage over the other infielders in that he has fewer throws to make after fielding a grounder and rarely has to hurry a long throw.

Before every pitch, he must evaluate the situation in order to know what action to take on any batted ball. Thorough preparation will prevent many costly mistakes.

Teaming with the pitcher. Since the pitcher covers first on all balls hit to the left of the mound, the first baseman, upon fielding the ball, must decide if he can make the putout unassisted. If he can, he should immediately wave the pitcher off. He should then hustle to first, step on the infield side of the base, and turn immediately toward the infield to avoid colliding with the runner.

When fielding the ball close to the foul line, however, he may have to run across the base into foul territory. If there are runners on base, he should then turn immediately toward the infield, ready to make another play.

If he cannot make the putout unassisted, he must throw to the pitcher, covering. As soon as he fields the ball, he should pull his glove hand away and deliver the ball to the pitcher.

If he is close to the base, he should step toward the pitcher and toss the ball underhanded (Fig. 10-6). The throw should reach the pitcher chest-high, two or three steps from the base, so that he can easily make the catch and tag the base.

One of the first baseman's toughest plays occurs when he is uncertain whether the pitcher will be able to field a grounder. He must not assume that the pitcher will field the ball. He must start for the ball, evaluate the situation, and, if he can make the play, call for the ball. This instructs the pitcher to cover first base.

Fig. 10-6.

If the pitcher can make the play, he should call for the ball so that the first baseman can cover. When both players call, the pitcher should field it with the first baseman covering. Many hours of drill are required to master this tough play.

Sometimes the first baseman will bobble the ball, or the ball will be hit so slowly that the pitcher can reach the base before the first baseman is ready to throw. In this case the pitcher should stop, put one foot on the base, and step toward the thrower with the other foot. The first baseman should then throw overhand directly to the base.

Holding a baserunner on Base. In holding a runner on, the first baseman faces the pitcher with his right foot along the home-plate side of the base, his toes even with the corner, his left foot on the first base line, and his glove about three feet from the ground extended toward the pitcher (Fig. 10-7).

In this position he can take a throw just in front of the base and merely drop his glove to the ground to complete the tag. He lets the runner come to him; he does not go after him. If the runner does not slide, the first baseman tries to touch the tagging foot.

If the runner on first is not likely to steal, the first baseman sometimes moves off the base behind the runner to prevent the ball from being hit down the line (Fig. 10-8). When the pitch is delivered,

Fig. 10-7.

Fig. 10-8.

he may back up a step or two from this position.

Whenever the first baseman decides to change positions, he should inform the pitcher accordingly to prevent a balk or a wild throw.

On a bunt situation with runners on first and second, the first baseman plays in front of the runner, usually on the edge of the grass (Fig. 10-9). He also plays in close on an anticipated squeeze play.

Fig. 10-9.

Throwing. As noted earlier, the first baseman need not have as strong an arm as the other infielders. His throwing ability is important, however, and if he has a strong arm, so much the better.

The first baseman must know what type of throw to use in every situation. The throw to second is generally made overhand because it has more carry and is more accurate. When the throw must be made quickly, however, the sidearm delivery is used. If the ball is fielded on the infield grass, the throw should be made to the infield side of second; if it is fielded behind the baseline, the throw should be to the outfield side.

The first baseman's throws to the plate are usually short, since they usually are made when the infield is playing in. He must get the throw off quickly and accurately. The way to develop quick and accurate throwing is to concentrate on making *every* practice throw a perfect one.

Cut-Off Plays. Almost all the other first-baseman throws stem from cut-off plays. The number of cut-off plays involving the first baseman will depend largely on the system employed by the coach.

In most cut-off systems, the first baseman serves as the "cut" man on all throws to the plate except on singles to left field. This method seems to provide the most complete coverage for all bases. For simplicity some coaches use the first baseman as the cut-off man on *all* throws to the plate.

There are advantages to both systems, but for the most thorough coverage of all bases on a single, the third baseman is used on any ball hit to left. The latter set-up also enables the defense to trap the batter as he rounds first. This will not provide coverage at first on singles to right and center fields on which the second baseman cannot cover. But the outfielders, by keeping their throws low, can prevent the runners from advancing.

The first baseman should hold his hands high above his head as a target whenever he is in the cut-off position so that the outfielders will be able to see him more easily.

Defensing the Bunt. On an anticipated bunt with a runner on first, the first baseman charges toward the plate as the pitcher starts his delivery. This run should not be straight down the line; the first two steps should be taken at a 45° angle into the infield. Hence, if the ball is bunted hard and to the first baseman's right, he is in position to field it and go for the force play at second.

If the ball is bunted in front of him, he fields it and throws to the base called by the catcher.

If the first baseman knows he cannot get the batter on a slow bunt down the line, he should permit the ball to roll if there is a chance that it may go foul. With a runner on, the first baseman must be alert to prevent him from taking an extra base. On a bunt in foul territory close to the line, the first baseman should touch it as quickly as possible to keep it from rolling fair.

Whenever possible the first baseman should cover first on all bunts toward third. Whenever the catcher must cover third, the first baseman should be alert to cover the plate. Whenever the first baseman is unable to get back to cover first, the second baseman assumes this duty.

POINTS TO REMEMBER

The first baseman should:
1. Get to the base as quickly as possible to shift right or left for the throw.
2. Present a target to the inside of the base whenever the

catcher, pitcher, or third baseman is throwing from the plate area.

3. Carry his hands low in fielding grounders.
4. *Always expect a bad throw.* Good throws are easy to catch.
5. Field grounders in front of his body.
6. Leave the base to catch extra-wide throws.
7. Team with the pitcher, if necessary, to make the putout.
8. Hold the runner close on an anticipated steal.
9. When charging a bunt with a runner on first, take the first two steps at a 45° angle into the infield.
10. On a bunt toward third, cover first, if possible, and, after getting the ball, rush toward any runner hung up between bases.
11. On a dropped third strike, present a target in foul territory, as the ball will usually go behind the catcher.
12. Let the catcher know when a runner is stealing.
13. Cover the area up to the pitcher's mound on any bunt attempt to advance a runner from second to third.
14. Back up the second baseman on all throws from left field.
15. Use two hands in fielding, whenever possible.
16. On a ground ball or throw to the plate side of first with a runner on third, run the batter-runner back toward the plate if he pulls up, to help prevent the runner from scoring.
17. Step toward second base in making a throw for a force out.
18. Throw to the infield side of second base for a force out when the ball has been fielded on the infield grass.
19. Work a pitchout with the catcher, if the runner can be caught off first.
20. Make no move to shift feet until the ball is in flight to him.

11

PLAYING THE KEYSTONE

Baseball experts are quick to agree that the success of a baseball team lies in its strength down the middle. So as the coach builds his club, a great deal of time must be spend developing the keystone combination—the shortstop and the second baseman. These two players form the heart of the defense. Efficient keystone play depends on their ability to work as a unit. Their teamwork is very important, since each covers the base under different circumstances, and when either is not covering, he has to perorm some related duty. This means that the shortstop and the second baseman must learn to work together and to react as a team whenever a ball is hit or a runner tries to advance. Very few teams have achieved championship heights without a smooth-working, dependable, double play combination.

SECOND BASEMAN

Qualifications: This position does not require any special size, but it does demand a good arm and good speed. Since the second baseman must serve as the pivot man on many double plays, he must have agility, quick mental reactions, and the ability to throw from any position. No other player on the team will make as many different types of throws as a good second baseman. Quickness is a second baseman's greatest asset.

Making the Double Play: The second baseman may shift his feet several ways at second base to catch the ball for a force-out and throw to first base.

As soon as the ball is hit, he must move to the base as quickly as possible and assume a set position. This gives the shortstop a stationary target and enables the second baseman to receive the throw and to shift in any direction. The pivot should *not* be made on the run—the feet should be set for the throw to first. One of the simplest pivots to teach and a very effective way to evade the baserunner is for the second baseman to step on the base with his left foot (Fig. 11-1), and then into the diamond with his right foot (Fig. 11-2) to make the throw (Fig. 11-3).

Fig. 11-1.

Fig. 11-2.

Fig. 11-3.

If the feeding throw is accurate and the runner is far enough away, the baseman can step on the base with his right foot (Fig. 11-4) just as he catches the ball, and then step toward first base with his left foot for the throw (Fig. 11-5).

Fig. 11-4.   Fig. 11-5.

If the runner is close and on the infield side of the base line, the second baseman may place his left foot on the outfield side of second base to make the catch (Fig. 11-6), then push back to his right foot, and step toward first with his left foot to complete the throw (Fig. 11-7).

If the throw to second goes to the second baseman's right, he steps on the left field side of the base with his left foot and out with his right foot to make the catch. He then shifts his weight to the right foot and steps toward first with the left for the throw.

If the throw is to the second baseman's left, he places his right foot on the home-plate corner of the base and steps out to his left with his left foot for the catch. If the runner is close, the baseman must step forward with the right foot after the catch, out of the way of the runner, and then toward first with the left foot for his throw.

If the second baseman can get to the base quickly enough, he may straddle it (Fig. 11-8). Then, if the throw is accurate, he can step out toward first with his left foot and drag his right toe against the left-field side of the base for the throw (Fig 11-9).

Fielding and Throwing to Second: Whenever the second baseman

Fig. 11-6.

Fig. 11-7.

Fig. 11-8.

Fig. 11-9.

is called upon to throw to second for a force-out, he should try to make his footwork as simple as possible.

After fielding a ground ball to his left, he should pivot to his right on his left foot, swing the right foot behind the left, and then step out with his left foot toward second to complete the throw.

If he can come to a full stop and set himself, he should pivot on his right foot and step toward second with his left foot for the throw. He should not stand upright, but remain in a semi-squat for the pivot. As he throws, he may rise slightly, but the faster he must make the play, the less he should raise his body.

After fielding a grounder while moving toward second, the baseman should immediately pull his gloved hand away so that the shortstop can see the ball. Then, using only the forearm and wrist, he can toss the ball underhand to the shortstop (Fig. 11-10).

If only a step or two from the base, the baseman should step on it

Fig. 11-10.

for the force-out, and then make the throw to first himself. This action can be performed quickly and will eliminate the chance of an error on a toss. Whenever the baseman can make the play, he should call "I've got it!", to prevent the shortstop from interfering with him.

Upon fielding a ground ball hit directly to him, the baseman should pivot to the right on the balls of both feet, so that the toes point toward second, and then make the throw (Fig. 11-11). This usually is a short, overhand snap from a squat. For a longer throw, the baseman will have to use more body, arm, and leg power.

Fig. 11-11.

On a ground ball fielded directly behind second, the baseman may backhand the ball to the shortstop from the gloved hand. This can be done only, of course, from a short distance.

Playing a Bunt: The second baseman sets up close to first so that he can cover first in the event the first baseman is unable to do so. Unless he has a pick-off play with the catcher, the second baseman should hold this position until the ball is bunted or until the pitch passes the batter. Leaving too soon will open a hole in the defense. In order not to leave a hole in the defense, the second baseman can advance toward the plate until the ball is bunted. Such an advance shortens the distance to first also.

Upon reaching first, the baseman should place his left foot on the second-base side of the base and his right foot into the diamond, giving the fielder a good target. As soon as he makes the put-out, he should turn into the diamond, alert for a possible play at third. Whenever the first baseman covers for the throw, the second baseman should back him up.

When a bunt is expected with men on first and second, the second baseman should always cover first, since the first baseman will be playing in for a possible force at third. In this case, the second baseman should (after taking the throw) be alert for a possible play at the plate.

With a runner on second only, the play is made the same as with a runner on first.

Balls to the Outfield: The second baseman covers second on all balls hit to left until he is certain the shortstop can cover. He then backs up the throw from the outfielder.

The second baseman generally takes all relays on balls to right field. As the ball is hit, he swings toward second, watching the outfielder making the play. If the ball is fielded cleanly, he receives the throw from the fielder. If the throw is wide, he runs toward it, acting as cut-off man, while the shortstop comes in to cover.

If the ball passes the outfielder, the second baseman runs toward him, at the same time listening for instructions from the shortstop. He runs to a position on line with the throw and close enough to permit the relay to be caught on the fly.

After catching the ball, he turns to his left to make his throw. If the runner stops at second or third, the second baseman, after catching the ball, should run toward the infield, ready to throw on an attempted advance.

When first base is occupied, the second baseman should cover second on any single to right field that is fielded cleanly. The throw will go to third base. If it is wide or too late to catch the runner attempting to reach third, the shortstop will cut it off and possibly make a play on the batter-runner. Should the lead runner make a long turn at second, the second baseman will be in position for a play from the shortstop.

The second baseman, hence, covers second on all hits to right except those past the right fielder. On open fields, such hits usually will be good for at least three bases, so the second baseman must go out and line up the throw to the plate.

Fly Balls in the Infield: When the first baseman fields a foul or fair fly ball with a man on first, the second baseman must cover first. This also holds true on a fair fly ball with no one on first.

When the second baseman fields a fly ball back of him with a man on base, he should immediately run toward the infield to prevent the runner from attempting to advance. This is particularly true with third base occupied.

When the shortstop fields a fly ball, the second baseman covers second. When the shortstop and third baseman go after a flv ball with a man on second, the second baseman covers third, unless the pitcher does so.

Ground Balls: The second baseman should try for any slow or medium-hit ground ball to his left. As soon as he is sure he can make the play, he should call to the first baseman, running him back to first for the throw. The second baseman is in better position to make the play, since he is moving in the direction of his throw.

When the ball is fielded in the area of the plate with the first baseman covering his base, the second baseman backs up the throw. He also backs up second whenever the shortstop covers the base on a throw from the plate area.

On grounders to his right, the second baseman should try to get in front of the ball, stopping squarely in front of it and bracing on his right leg. The braced leg furnishes a firm support for the subsequent throw.

SHORTSTOP

Qualifications: The shortstop should have a good pair of hands, a strong arm and quickness. He must be able to charge slow-hit ground balls and to move right or left for the hard ground balls. Baseball sense and anticipation are also valuable assets, and height, though not essential, is an advantage.

Making the Double Play: As soon as the ball is hit, the shortstop should get to the base as quickly as possible and assume a set position for the throw and target. As emphasized at second base, the pivot should not be made on the run, if possible.

The simplest and most popular pivot presents itself when the throw is received a step to the outfield side of the base. The right foot is placed on the right-field side of the base as he steps out with his left foot for the catch (Fig. 11-12). He then brings his right foot behind the left and steps toward first with his left for the throw (Fig. 11-13). These steps will carry him well away from the runner.

If the throw is to his right, the shortstop places his left foot on the third-base side of the base and steps out with his right to receive the throw (Fig. 11-14). He then pivots on his right foot and steps into the diamond with his left foot for the throw (Fig. 11-15).

When time permits, the shortstop may straddle the base and make his throw in front of the slider. As he receives the ball, he places his left foot on the right-field side of the base, then brings his right foot over the base, and steps out with his left for the throw. If the runner

Fig. 11-12.

Fig. 11-13.

Fig. 11-14.

Fig. 11-15.

is close, the step with the left foot should be away from him.

Many experts consider the leap-flip as the fastest way to make the double play, although it is the hardest to learn. The shortstop hits the base with his right foot and makes a flat flip throw to first, jumping in the air to avoid the runner.

The throw to the shortstop from the catcher or pitcher should be made to the base, chest high. If he is moving, the throw should be slightly toward the third-base side. The shortstop usually will take this throw on the run and, as he catches the ball, step on the base.

If he steps on the base with his right foot, he must use the base as a pivot in stepping out with his left foot for the throw. If he steps on base with his left foot as he makes the catch, he should step toward first with his right foot and then with his left for the throw The step should be away from the runner (toward the inside of the diamond) if the play is close.

Fielding and Throwing to Second: Upon fielding a ground ball with a double play in order, the shortstop ordinarily should not straighten up; he should throw from the position in which he fields the ball.

On a ground ball directly at him, he may take a short step with his left foot in the direction of his throw, at the same time pulling his gloved hand down and away as he makes a snap overhand throw (Fig. 11-16)

He will sometimes be called upon to throw from a squat position, using only arm action. In this case he would not take a step, but would pivot left on the balls of his feet so that his toes point in the direction of his throw.

Upon fielding a ground ball to his left (close to the base), he should pull his gloved hand away from the ball to show it, and then toss underhand to second, using a wrist and forearm snap rather than a full-arm swing (Fig. 11-17).

If the shortstop is only a step or two from the base as he catches the ball, he should call, "I've got it!", and make the play himself. The call is necessary to prevent the second baseman from coming into the base and interfering with the play.

On a ground ball to his right, the shortstop should move into position as quickly as possible, stopping squarely in front of the ball by bracing his right leg. He should throw immediately after fielding the ball as he will rarely have time to straighten up. He will usually have to use a snap overhand or sidearm throw, depending on the position in which he fielded the ball. If he finds a step with his left foot is necessary, he should make it short and in the direction of the throw.

Playing the Bunt: With first occupied and a bunt anticipated, the

Fig. 11-16.

Fig. 11-17.

shortstop should move closer to second (double-play position) to facilitate his coverage.

With first and second occupied, no one out, the shortstop holds the runner close to second for a possible force at third. He should set up no more than two or three steps behind the base. As the pitcher delivers, he should move over to cover his normal position, unless the batter drops his bat for a bunt. With two strikes on the batter, the shortstop should take his double-play position.

Balls to the Outfield: On a single to right with no one on base, the shortstop covers second until the second baseman comes over to cover. He then backs up the throw to the base.

On a single to left, he covers the base if the ball is fielded cleanly. If the throw is wide, he leaves the base for the cutoff.

On a single to right with a man on first, the shortstop runs to a cutoff position for the throw to third. If the throw is made to second, he backs it up. On throws to third, the shortstop is given instruction by the third baseman. If the latter calls "Cut!", the shortstop looks for a play on the back runner—looking for an attempted advance to second or a wide turn at first.

On a single to left with a man on first, the shortstop lines up with the throw to third, about 15 to 20 yards from the base. If the throw is wide, he cuts it off and looks for a possible play on the back runner.

When second or third is occupied, the shortstop covers third on base hits and fly balls to the outfield, while the third baseman acts as the cut-off man.

The shortstop usually takes all relays on balls hit past the left and center fielders. As the ball is hit, he swings toward second, watching the play. If the hit is a single that can be fielded cleanly, he takes the throw from the outfielder.

If the ball passes the outfielder, he runs toward him, at the same time listening for direction from the second baseman. He hustles to a position in line with the outfielder's throw and the base to which he will throw. He should be close enough to catch the relay on the fly. After catching the ball, he should turn to his left to make the throw.

Fly Balls in the Infield: The shortstop covers second on all fly balls taken by the second baseman, and third on all fly balls taken by the third baseman. The shortstop should take most fly balls hit directly behind the third baseman, as he is in better position to handle the ball by not having to turn and run backward.

Ground Balls: The shortstop should move in as fast as possible on all ground balls his way to save time and cut down the length of the throws. Playing a ball too slow is a common fault among inexperienced shortstops.

With second occupied and fewer than two outs, the shortstop should, on a ground ball hit sharply to him or to his right, glance at the runner and fake him back to the base before throwing to first. With two outs, the play is normally made to first.

If, with second base occupied, the shortstop fumbles a ball and the runner advances, he should be alert for a possible play at third; a quick throw can pick off any runner making a long turn.

The shortstop covers second on all grounders hit to the first-base side of second and in the home plate and pitcher's area, except when his position makes it impossible.

When the third baseman goes in for a slow roller with a man on first, the shortstop covers third, unless the catcher or pitcher gets there first.

POINTS TO REMEMBER

The Keystone combination should:
1. Use mouth signals to decide who will cover second on some straight-away hitters.
2. Employ a verbal sign to inform the first and third baseman of a slow ball or change of pace.
3. Use a closed fist for a fast ball, an open hand for a curve, and a wiggle of the fingers for a change-up in signalling pitches to the outfield.
4. Stretch for the force-out at second whenever the double play cannot be made, as well as when there are two outs.
5. Be alert to retrieve an errant catcher's throw to the pitcher.
6. Call "I have it!" if you can make the force-out at second unassisted, so that your teammate will not interfere with the play.
7. Call "Cut!" to the cutoff man if the throw to second is wide or if the runner cannot be retired. No call means do not intercept the ball.
8. Take a position approximately 100 to 150 feet from an outfielder when acting as a relay man. Spin toward the glove hand and throw to the base on a hop.
9. Stand just in front of second when handling the catcher's peg on a first-and-third steal. Break in to take the throw if the runner on third attempts to score, unless it is more important to catch the runner advancing from first.
10. Make long relay throws to third and home on a hop.
11. Practice the double-team pickoff play. The player designated to cover fakes the pickoff, then the other player breaks for the base.
12. Move in a step or two with a man on first to increase the chances for a double play.

13. Always make sure of the first out.
14. Take a step or two toward second after the ball has passed the batter with a runner on first. This prevents a delayed steal.
15. Position themselves for the hit-and-run with a runner on first and the pitcher behind the hitter.
16. Move two steps in with men on first and third and the count at 3-1 or 3-2; this is a double-steal situation.
17. Ignore the man on third unless he is the tying or winning run with men on first and third.
18. Always decide who will do what before the next play.
19. Use a quick snap throw, letter high, to the pivot man.
20. Get to the base quickly if you are the pivot man, and use any extra time to coordinate the pivot.

12

PLAYING THE HOT CORNER

Playing third base, commonly known as the hot corner, requires sharp reflexes and quick thinking. The third baseman should possess a strong, accurate throwing arm and have the ability to throw from any position in which he fields the ball. Running speed is not essential, but quick reactions, a sure pair of hands, and the ability to handle the ball quickly are important. A successful third baseman must be able to charge in fast on slowly-hit and bunted balls. Since his fielding position often brings him close to the batter, hard-hit balls sometimes cannot be fielded cleanly. He must, therefore, be able to block such batted balls and have the agility to retrieve them in time to throw out the batter-runner.

TECHNIQUES OF THIRD BASE PLAY

The third baseman's position probably is more versatile than that of any other infielder. Mental alertness to each possible play situation helps to make an outstanding third baseman. When the bases are unoccupied with fewer than two outs, he must anticipate a possible bunt for a base hit. If he suspects a bunt he must play in closer than his normal position until two strikes are called on the batter. This close position may be anywhere from even with third base to five feet ahead of the baseline between second and third bases, depending on his knowledge of the batter.

Fielding Ground Balls. The third baseman must be ready at all times for ground balls in his direction. It is very important that he crouches as low as possible, since he will get a better angle on the ball and can follow it more readily (Fig. 12-1). From this position, he takes a half step just as the ball is being delivered by the pitcher so he will be moving slowly forward when the ball is hit. It is important that the third baseman expects every ball to be hit to him and that he knows what to do when he fields it.

The third baseman advances as fast as possible on all slowly-hit

189

Fig. 12-1.

and bunted balls which he attempts to handle. He fields the ball in front of his right foot, as his left foot comes down on the ground (Fig. 12-2). The ball should be fielded with both hands whenever possible. He should make the throw while straightening up, with his body still moving forward, and turning toward first base. Some college players can make the underhand throw, but most coaches think the barehand scoop and underhand throw are for professionals.

There is a method of fielding the slow-hit ball which has stopped rolling without taking it into the glove or using the bare-hand scoop. The third baseman picks it up on the side of his glove (Fig. 12-3). This method has been very successful at Lipscomb.

If the ball is bunted or hit slowly close to the third base line and is foul, it should be touched immediately. If the ball is fair, and the batter-runner cannot be thrown out, it should be permitted to roll, since there is a chance it will roll foul. However, if a runner is on base and will be able to advance while the ball is rolling, it should be picked up to keep the base runner from advancing.

The third baseman should attempt to field all ground balls which he can reach to his left. He is in better position to make the play than the shortstop. If the shortstop can make the play on the hard-hit ground ball, he should call it, to eliminate the possibility of

Fig. 12-2.

Fig. 12-3.

the ball being deflected by the third baseman.

When first base is occupied and the third baseman fields a ground ball hit to his left, the throw should be to second base, provided he has time to make the play. This is a shorter throw than to first base, and he has his body moving in that direction.

When second base is occupied and there are fewer than two outs, the third baseman should "look the runner back" at second base after he fields a hard-hit ground ball. This forces the runner to stay close to the base. The same should be done to a runner on third base. He will still have time to throw to first.

If there are runners on first and third base, no outs, and a close score on a ball hit hard to the third baseman, he takes a quick look at the runner on third base. If he attempts to score, the throw is made immediately to the plate. If the runner does not break when the ball is hit, the third baseman makes his play to second base. Frequently with one out, the play goes to second for the double play from second to first. This strategy is used when the first and third baseman are playing in and when the shortstop and second baseman are playing back. With several runs ahead and fewer than two outs, the throw should always go to second base for the double play, which lessens the chances of a big inning.

If second and third bases are occupied, one out, score close, most teams will attempt to have both runners advance on a ground ball to the third baseman. The play then is made to the catcher. With no outs, some teams will not attempt to advance unless the ball is hit slowly to the third baseman. In this situation he must decide if he has a play at home plate.

When the third baseman has a play at the plate, he should throw the ball to the catcher as quickly as possible. Then he should break over and down the base line for a possible rundown, if the runner stops and attempts to return to third base. The catcher can make a quick throw to the third baseman who can tag the runner retreating to third base. If the runner from second base has advanced to third and the runner in the rundown makes it back, the runner from second should be tagged. The runner who first occupied the base is entitled to it. To avoid confusion, both runners should be tagged.

Sacrifice Bunt. When the sacrifice bunt is anticipated by the third baseman, he should watch the batter very closely; if the batter shifts the bat forward to bunt, he should charge toward home plate. If the batter draws his bat back, the third baseman should stop abruptly, anticipating a swing.

The position of the third baseman before he charges home plate is about five feet wide of third base and on the edge of the infield grass (Fig. 12-4). From this position, he will go straight in on the ball

Fig. 12-4.

when he fields it. If someone else fields the bunt, the third baseman should return immediately to third base.

When first and second bases are occupied and a bunt is expected, the third baseman assumes a position not more than five steps from the third base. The pitcher covers the third base side of the diamond by moving directly toward the foul line, while the third baseman stays close to the base for a possible force-out. The third baseman must be alert to field a ball bunted so hard that the pitcher cannot handle it. In this situation he should field the ball and make his throw to first base. If the batter attempts to hit, the third baseman breaks several steps to the left of his base, prepared to field a ball hit in his area.

When a runner is on second, the third baseman must be careful not to leave his position too quickly, leaving the base unprotected against a steal. Some teams will fake bunt and steal in this situation. With two strikes on the batter, the third baseman usually can return to his normal position, depending on the batter. Some poor-hitting pitchers may attempt a sacrifice bunt with two strikes on them.

Handling Pop-Flies. The third baseman should take all fly balls between third base and home plate. He is in much better position to take fly balls in this area, and he should "run the catcher off" by calling loud and clear for the ball. The third baseman and the first baseman must also field pop-flies in the area of the mound, since this is a difficult play for the pitcher.

The shortstop is in better position to handle pop-flies behind third base and should call for the ball, so the third baseman will know he can make the play.

The third baseman covers third when second base is occupied and a fly ball is hit which he himself does not attempt to field. He does the same with third base occupied except when the catcher fields a fly ball and the pitcher or first baseman leaves home plate uncovered. In this case, the third baseman covers home, and the shortstop covers third base.

Throwing. The third baseman should throw overhanded to first base whenever possible. An overhand throw is generally faster and certainly more likely to be accurate. A ball thrown sidearm has a tendency to sail away and down. It is recommended that young players practice fielding ground balls and bringing themselves into a position immediately to throw overhand.

In throwing, the grip of the baseball is very important to get maximum carry on it and to eliminate the possibility of its sailing. It should be gripped with the tips of the first two fingers and the thumb across the seams. Most major league third basemen favor gripping the ball across the seams. As the arm is brought back for the throw, the player can switch his fingers to the correct position without looking at the ball.

Because of the variety of plays the third baseman has to handle, he must be proficient in throwing sidearm and underhand, as well as overhand.

The throw to second base to start a double play is of the utmost importance. The ball must reach the second baseman chest high and directly over the base. The third baseman should use a semi-crouch position and throw overhand to the base, if he must hurry his throw (Fig. 12-5). If the ball reaches him before the second baseman has time to get in position for the play, he can stand up and time his overhand throw to reach the base as the second baseman arrives. In some situations he will be forced to throw underhand or sidearm to the second baseman because of the speed of the ball and the position in which he finds himself.

If the ball is hit near the base with first and second occupied, the

Fig. 12-5.

third baseman should touch third base and throw to first for the double play. When the bases are loaded, the third baseman should go home with the ball for the force-out, and the catcher can go to first for the double play. In professional baseball the play usually is made at second base to execute the double play, but in amateur baseball, it usually is best to be sure the runner does not score. Again, if the ball is hit near the base, the third baseman should touch the base and go home with the ball, letting the catcher know the force is off at the plate and the runner must be tagged.

Receiving Throws. The third baseman should straddle the base, facing the direction the throw is coming from, with his feet several inches behind the front edge of it. If the throw is wide, he is in good position to go to either side of the base to make the catch.

When the throw comes from the catcher on an attempted steal, the third baseman should straddle the back part of the base, with his body turned slightly toward the catcher (Fig. 12-6). This leaves the

Fig. 12-6.

base open for the runner and avoids the possibility of his interfering with the third baseman. As he catches the ball, he makes the tag by turning left slightly and facing the runner. If the throw is wide, he is in good position to go to either side to make the catch. If he must leave the base to catch the ball, he does so.

When there is a runner on second base and third base is open, the third baseman should develop the habit of taking a step toward third base after the ball passes the batter. He should glance at the runner while he is taking this step. If this is done, he will always be in position to cover the base on an attempt to steal.

When a runner is leading off third base, his lead is normally in foul territory; therefore, the catcher must throw to the second base side of third base for a pick-off play. If the throw is accurate, there is little danger of the runner being hit. As the third baseman catches the ball he should step across the base with his right foot, facing the runner as he makes the tag.

When the third baseman receives a throw on a force-out, he should place his right foot on the corner of the base closest to the pitcher's mound and stretch forward with his left foot in the direction of the throw (Fig. 12-7).

Fig. 12-7.

Basically, there are two ways of tagging a base runner. One way is to bring the glove down in front of the base and then look for the runner's foot, tagging it with the back of the glove. It is important here that the infielder does not allow the runner to knock the ball out of his glove hand. Some infielders will smother the ball with both hands to prevent this. In this situation, the glove should be held a few inches away from the base so there is room to absorb the contact of the runner's foot.

The second way to tag a base runner is by sweeping the ball across the line of his slide. In receiving the throw, the third baseman sweeps the ball in an arc down across his foot and up again. If he has to wait, he does not plant his glove but holds it cocked to one side and times his sweep. When the base runner slides, he snaps the glove hand down and across his foot.

Base-Covering and Cut-Off Duties. When first base is occupied and a base hit goes to the outfield, the third baseman covers his base.

If it is to right field and the base runner continues on to third base, the third baseman should give instructions to the shortstop to cut-off the throw if it is wide or late. Then he should try to make a play after he has cut-off the throw.

When the third baseman is designated as the cutoff man on base hits or fly balls into left field, he should place himself approximately sixty feet from home plate and in line with the outfielder. When he reaches this position, he should raise both arms into the air, so the outfielder can easily locate the cutoff man (Fig. 12-8). If the throw is wide or late, the catcher instructs the third baseman to cut-off the throw and alerts him for a possible play on the batter-runner.

Fig. 12-8.

POINTS TO REMEMBER

Some "Points to Remember" are basic rules for an aggressive third baseman:

1. Check the terrain around third base before the game starts.
2. Always watch the hitter, not the pitcher, when the pitch is being delivered to the batter. This enables a better jump on the ball and aids in early detection of a bunt.
3. With two out, guard the foul line in an effort to prevent an extra base hit.

4. When any base is occupied, back up throws from the first baseman to the pitcher.

5. Block hard-hit balls, because the batter may very often be thrown out at first base even though the ball is not fielded cleanly.

6. Attempt to field any ball to your left because this position usually is a difficult chance for the shortstop.

7. Listen for the catcher's voice if in doubt where to make a throw.

8. Think ahead on every play and study the opposing hitters.

9. Give way to the shortstop on fly balls back of third base.

10. When the bases are loaded, make the double play home to first.

11. Be alert for a squeeze play with third occupied and fewer than two outs in a close ball game.

12. Permit slow-hit balls along the foul line to roll when the batter cannot be retired at first.

13. Field bunts and slow hit balls with two hands, if possible.

14. Cover third base unless you are required to perform some other duty on defense.

15. With runners on first and second, go for the double play by way of second, unless the ball is hit close to the base.

16. Be alert for a fake bunt with second base occupied. This may be a planned play to help the runner steal third.

17. Take the cut-off position for throws to the plate after a single to left field with a runner in scoring position.

18. Never back up on balls hit directly at you, since this in effect allows the ball to play you.

19. Watch each runner rounding the base on his way home and check the men tagging up to score after a fly ball is caught. Call for an appeal play if the runner misses the base or leaves too soon on a fly ball.

20. Call "Cut" to the shortstop if a throw to third base is wide or if the runner cannot be retired. No call means, "Let the ball go."

13

THE SPACE PATROL

Many outfielders habitually stand around in the field as though playing in the outfield were a stationary job. On the contrary, an efficient outfielder practices the meaning of the word "hustle" and moves to a correct position on every play either in the infield or the outfield. He is alert and quick in backing up other players on all balls thrown or batted in his direction. He must be able to catch flies, liners, grounders, and balls hit over his head and to make low, hard throws. A strong throwing arm, speed, and intelligence—all are essentials for a successful outfielder.

Tireless practice of certain techniques will increase his effectiveness.

Stance. Outfielders use two basic stances: the "square" and the "drop-step". In the "square" stance, used also by infielders, the outfielder faces the hitter, his feet parallel and comfortably separated, with his weight on the balls of his feet (Fig. 13-1). In the "drop-step", the outfielder also faces the batter, but he places the toe of the rear foot even with the heel of the front foot (Fig. 13-2). The expected direction of the ball determines which foot is dropped back. This position enables the player to get a quicker jump on the ball. The "drop-step", which allows an easy backward or forward movement, is the one more frequently used today. In either stance, the foot farthest from the ball generally takes the first step, a cross-over in the direction of the ball.

A frequent mistake of outfielders is keeping their hands on their knees when the pitcher delivers the ball. Although they may *rest* in this position, the hands should be lifted when the pitcher starts his wind-up, thus being ready to move in any direction.

Throwing. Throwing is another important skill. Every batter and every runner creates a different situation. The outfielder must prevent batters from taking that extra base as well as nail runners who overrun or tag-up.

Fig. 13-1.

Fig. 13-2.

The ideal outfield throw is low and fast. It should be made overhand and, unless the distance is short, should reach the base on one hop. The ball should be gripped across the seams to achieve the best carry and to eliminate curves.

All relay throws should reach the cutoff man chest high. If he gives the outfielder an accurate line, the ball should bounce or hop to the base or plate. Many coaches fail to impress upon the outfielder that he must hit the cutoff man with a low throw. If apparently the runner will reach base easily, the cutoff man still can make a play on another advancing runner. A low throw thus may enable him to change the direction of the play.

An outfielder should consider every possible play before each pitch is made. As each batter comes to the plate, he should survey the situation—men on base, outs, inning, score, the baserunners' habits, and the probable direction of the ball. After evaluating all the facts and possibilities and deciding upon the most logical procedure, he is ready. If he waits until the ball is on its way before determining the proper play, he will delay his throw and possibly throw to the wrong base.

An outfielder should remember that sometimes it is more advantageous to prevent a runner from getting into a scoring position than to keep another man from scoring. The percentage of putouts at the plate on outfield throws is small. The score, the inning, and the number of outs should be the important factors in making such a decision.

Fielding. The outfielder's primary job is catching flies and grounders cleanly. Line drives and flies hit directly over his head are his two most difficult plays.

On liners, he should keep his eyes on the ball constantly. If he is not sure about his first step, he should take one step backward. An inexperienced outfielder who takes a step forward when he is uncertain, often finds the ball carrying over his head. Constant practice is needed to curb the instinct to charge forward on all liners. It is understood, of course, that the outfielder will charge all balls that he is sure will remain in front of him.

In catching a fly hit over his head, an outfielder should turn and run to the spot where he thinks the ball will descend. If possible, he should get in front of the ball; if not, he should make the catch over his shoulder. Always he should run on the balls of his feet, not on his heels.

If an outfielder is weak on this play, he should glue his eyes on the ball from the time it leaves the bat; however, in practices, he should turn his back on all such plays until he perfects the technique. Having someone throw balls over the outfielder's head is a helpful practice drill.

There are two methods of fielding grounders—the infielder method, and the knee on the ground. The proper choice depends on the game situation and the ground conditions. If the winning run is on second base in a late inning, the outfielder must charge the grounder and try to make a play at the plate. This is a desperation play, a do-or-die effort.

If the tying run is scoring in this situation, the outfielder may throw to the plate, or, if the runner obviously cannot be headed off, to second base to keep the winning run from advancing to second. This choice will depend on the coach's philosophy, the number of outs, which is the home team, and where the ball is hit. The outfielder must therefore be as alert as the catcher or the infielders.

On a ground ball hit to the outfield with the bases empty, the outfielder should play it safe by blocking the ball with one knee on the ground, the one on the same side as the player's throwing arm—right-handed thrower—right knee (Fig. 13-3).

Fig. 13-3.

Whether an outfielder can come in fast enough to catch a ball in front of him creates another tough problem. When his team has a comfortable lead, even if there are runners in scoring position, sometimes it is advisable to make an attempt. The shoestring catch is a gamble, though, and outfielders should learn the art of blocking the ball when they cannot make the catch.

The left and right fielders should remember that the pulled ball will hook toward the foul line and the sliced ball will veer away from the batter's normal line of power.

Every outfielder is aware of the difficulty that arises when a fly is hit in "neutral" territory. This situation is underscored when a fly drops safely because each of the outfielders thought the other had it. The average fan does not realize how many games are lost by such popfly "hits" resulting from outfielders' indecisions. The logical way to eliminate such errors is for the outfielders to work together. When both arrive within reach of the ball, the man who first yells "I have it" takes the ball, and the other gives him the right of way.

If an outfielder and an infielder call at the same time, the outfielder is always given preference; but if the infielder calls first, the outfielder should allow him to make the play. If the outfielders remember these cardinal points, they will minimize this difficulty.

Since most parks have a sun field, it is very important for each outfielder to have some experience playing with the sun in his face. The wise coach will buy a few pairs of special baseball sun glasses, which fit around the head with an elastic band. The player need merely tap the peak of his cap for them to flip into place (Fig. 13-4). These sun glasses will increase an outfielder's chances of catching balls coming out of the sun.

Although outfielders do not serve as relay men, they can be of help on such plays. An outfielder not involved with retrieving the ball lines up approximately halfway between the infield relay man and the player picking up the ball. He must, however, avoid hiding the relay man from the thrower. He watches the runners and then instructs the relay man where to throw.

Similarly, if two outfielders are chasing the ball, the player who does not pick it up aids the other. All relay and cutoff men should hold their hands high so that the outfielder can readily see his target.

Backing up the Infield. The art of backing up on all thrown and batted balls in one of the most difficult for the outfielder to master.

First, the outfielder must be "heads up" whenever there are men on base and where there is a possibility of an infielder to infielder throw. Until he perfects this area of play, he can never hope to become an excellent outfielder.

With a man on first, for example, a fly ball is hit to the leftfielder. After the catch he throws it to the infielder covering second. Many

Fig. 13-4.

·believe that the other outfielders have nothing to do on this play, as there is only a slight possibility that the throw would get by both the shortstop and the second baseman. *But there is that possibility.* The rightfielder, therefore, should move in behind the second baseman and thus prevent an advance by the runner on a miscue. In the identical situation on a fly to right, the leftfielder should line up the play and back up second.

On a grounder, the outfielders should assume the infielder will miss the ball and go to back-up position.

The centerfielder should be the most skilled outfielder because he has the largest territory to cover. Exceptional running speed is the key to greatness in center field. The player with the strongest arm should be placed in right field to prevent the scoring play from second to home, or the extra base from second to third on a single to right field. The left fielder needs reasonable speed, a strong arm, and the ability to judge curving line drives.

Most professional outfielders use a large glove with long fingers and considerable webbing. It gives the outfielder a longer reach, and the webbing provides a pocket where the ball will not jump out.

Playing the outfield is not an easy job. Those individuals who have the desire to be outfielders must realize that excellence comes only from many hours of hard work.

POINTS TO REMEMBER

A good outfielder should:
1. Always play a grounder safely, blocking it if necessary, when the bases are empty.
2. Watch the opponents in batting practice and make an analysis of each hitter.
3. Check the wind and sun at the start of each inning.
4. Always run on his toes when catching a fly ball.
5. Know when a pitchout or pickoff is called, so that he can make a fast start to back up the play.
6. Never give up on a fly ball.
7. Try to face the ball when making the catch.
8. Know the speed of every runner.
9. Always throw ahead of the runner to prevent an advance.
10. Try to catch every fly on his throwing arm side.
11. Remember if a batted ball to right or left is curving, it always curves toward the foul line.
12. Know the score, the inning, the number of outs, and the strengths and weaknesses of the opponent.
13. Charge all grounders, even if intending merely to block them.
14. Move away from the pull position with two strikes on the hitter.
15. Never hold the ball with runners on base.
16. Make one-bounce throws to all bases except when in close range.
17. Back up all throws from one infielder to another.
18. Move with every pitch.
19. Take all flies which can be handled either by an infielder or an outfielder, except when the infielder calls first.
20. Work out in the infield to learn to handle grounders.

14

DEFENSIVE PLAYS
AND STRATEGY

A team is rarely stronger than its defense. To perfect individual skills and coordinate them into team play are the real essentials to defense as a whole. Each defensive player must have and use a comprehensive knowledge of various baseball situations and of other conditions on the field which affect his defensive play. He must keep the following facts in mind: the score, the inning, the count on the batter, the number of outs, and the capabilities of the offensive players.

Every defensive player should plan what he will do if the next pitch is hit to him, including a plan of action should he make an error. If each player thoughtfully reviews all the possible plays that can occur in a given play situation, he will not make mental mistakes. Defense is based upon two factors: 1. each player in the right place at the right time; 2. each player aware of what he must do with the ball when it is hit to him.

TEAM DEFENSE

The defensive positions of infielders and outfielders usually depend on the stage of the game and the ability of the batter. If the situation in the game warrants playing back with a straightaway hitter at bat, the defense plays deep and is concentrated toward the middle of the diamond. In defending against a righthanded pull batter or a lefthanded opposite-field batter, the defense swings toward the left-field line, and the left-field side of the defense plays deeper than the right. The defense is swung similarly toward the right field line for a lefthanded pull hitter or a righthanded opposite field hitter.

When the stage of the game warrants playing in for the purpose of making a play at the plate, the defense moves forward to a position where the infielders are on the base line or on the edge of the infield grass. It is here that one of the most frequent and most serious violations of sound defensive positioning is made. The practice of playing the infield in close to cut-off a run at the plate whenever the opposition has a man on third is definitely overused, sometimes to the point of folly. An attempt should be made to cut down the man at the plate only if a really important run is involved, never in the early innings when there is plenty of opportunity to get back the run. If the defense plays in, the opponent's .200 hitter becomes a .400 hitter, and the gates are opened for a big inning.

The "medium" position of the infield should be used during the middle innings when it is desirable to prevent a run, but not to the extent of leaving the infield vulnerable to ground balls that may go through and set up the big inning. In late innings the "medium" position is employed when the batter lacks speed, the runner on third is fast, a double-play situation exists, and the infield is capable of making the double-play. It must be kept in mind here that the infielders may play "deep", "medium" or "short" as individuals rather than as a unit. A widely used infield set-up is to have the shortstop and the second baseman at "medium" depth and the first and the third baseman "deep". It is frequent strategy also to play the first and the third baseman "in close" to make the play at the plate, while the shortstop and the second baseman stay in the medium position going for the double play.

When a team is being met for the first time and no advance information is available concerning the various players, each player is considered a pull hitter. Definite decisions often are reached in this matter by watching the pregame practice. In fact, batting practice should be watched, even though the team has been played previously or has been scouted, because there is always the possibility that some batter may reveal a flagrant weakness that has been overlooked. Also a recheck can then be made as to where the various players hit the ball. The watching should involve all players and coaches.

The forward and backward movement of the defense should be controlled by the coach because if players are allowed to shift for themselves, some may play in and others back under the same conditions. If possible, decisions should be made prior to the start of the game, so that the infielders and outfielders will know where to play as soon as the batter steps to the plate. The coach often will alter the position of various players during the course of the game, but because of his many duties it is impossible for him to do so throughout the game. For this reason it is important for the defensive players to know where each batter is likely to hit the ball and to move accordingly. This should be done as a unit to give the defense balance.

DEFENSIVE POSITIONS

First Baseman. Depending upon his ability to go right or left, the first baseman's normal position is eight to fifteen feet from the foul line, and fifteen to twenty-five feet back of the line between first and second base. The hitter's tendency to pull the ball must be taken into consideration. The first baseman plays on the base with first or first and third bases occupied, except when a runner is not likely to attempt a steal. In this case, the first baseman stands a few steps behind the runner.

Infielders. the second baseman's normal position is twenty—to thirty feet back of the line between first and second base; the shortstop's is the same distance back of the line between second and third base. The third baseman's position is ten to twenty feet back of the line between second and third base.

The third baseman plays in the short position when a sacrifice bunt is expected with fewer than two outs and until two strikes are called against the batter who might bunt. He should play in this position also when a weak-hitting pitcher has two strikes charged against him, and the situation warrants a bunt. The first and the second baseman may move a few steps toward the batter for the same reason. If a bunt is attempted to move a runner to third base, the first baseman plays a few steps in front of the short position, and the shortstop stays close to second base to shorten the lead of the runner.

When there is a possibility of a steal of second base, the shortstop and the second baseman must agree on who will cover the base. The player covering should move in two or three steps toward the batter and a few steps toward second base. This position permits delaying the start to cover until the ball is hit or passes the batter. It also places the player in position to cover quickly on a delayed steal.

If an intentional pass is being issued, the player who normally covers second base takes a deep position, and the other player who forms the keystone combination plays on the base. This protects against a careless pitch, in which case the ball is more likely to be hit to the opposite field.

Double Play Defense. In a double play situation, the same pattern of shifts for each type of hitter should be followed, but the infield plays closer to the batter.

The shortstop and the second baseman move a few steps nearer the plate and second base to increase the chances for a double play. The only exception is a batter who definitely is known as a pull hitter. In this situation, the fielder on the side to which the batter hits plays the batter, placing himself somewhat deeper than for a normal double play.

The first baseman's position varies from approximately ten feet behind the first-to-second-base line to five feet ahead of that line. If he is holding a runner on first base, he should break toward second base as the pitch is delivered.

The third baseman plays from approximately ten feet behind the second-to-third-base line all the way to the line, depending upon the type of hitter. A strong pull hitter requires a deeper defensive position than a straightaway hitter.

Other Factors. Each player takes a defensive position according to his own fielding ability. If an infielder cannot go to the right as well as to the left or vice versa, he should play a few steps to the weak side. For a similar reason a slow outfielder plays deeper than one having speed. The inability to go back for balls is another weakness against which some outfielders must protect themselves.

The power and speed of the batter are also taken into consideration. When known hard hitters are batting, the defense plays deep, and if known weak hitters are at the plate, the infield moves in closer. This is doubly true for outfielders because of the large areas they must cover. The infielders must consider the speed with which the batter reaches first base. Fast, quick-breaking players are not played as deeply as those who are slow in reaching the base. Most lefthanded batters come under the fast group, since they bat from a position closer to first base.

In some cases the defensive positions are influenced by the pitcher's control and speed. A pitcher who depends on the fast ball for success usually causes the batter to hit late. On the other hand, the pitcher who relies on curves and control will find the batter pulling the ball most of the time.

The defensive position of the infielders may be affected by the condition of the field. Some infields are harder and faster than others and require a deeper defensive position. Some grass infields slow the ball down to such a degree that the infielders should play in a medium position. In the pre-game warm-up the defensive players should check the area they must cover. It is important to smooth rough places on the ground and remove obstacles such as rocks and paper. These may affect the fielding of ground balls.

THE RUN–DOWN

Every baseball team must have a planned defense against offensive players caught in a run-down. Many plans have merit, but the double and the single rotation will be discussed in this chapter.

In the double rotation system, the fundamental rule for the defense is always to follow their throw, except when the pitcher picks a runner off second base.

When the pitcher picks a runner off first base, he hustles to first and gets behind the base, since he will not be in the play, if executed properly. If it is not executed correctly, he will move up to the base, receive the ball, and tag the runner. The pitcher should stay out of the play if possible, because this minimizes the chance of injury.

As soon as the first baseman catches the ball, he should run toward the base runner. As soon as the shortstop is in position, the first baseman throws the ball to him and follows the throw to second base. The fundamental rule here is always to rotate to the right. The second baseman should go toward first base as soon as he sees the runner is picked off. He should cut in sharply behind the runner about fifteen feet from first base, in position to receive the throw from the shortstop. As soon as the shortstop receives the throw from the first baseman, he runs the runner toward first base as hard as he can. As the runner gets within a few feet of the second baseman, the throw is made by the shortstop. The second baseman may have to take a few steps forward quickly to tag the runner. Since the runner is going full speed toward first base, it will be impossible for him to stop and start in a new direction before being tagged out. If for some reason the runner gets by the second baseman, the throw should go to the pitcher, who is the spare man. When the shortstop throws to the second baseman or pitcher, he should continue on to first base, in case the runner is not retired. Two throws should be the maximum number to put a runner out.

If a runner has been picked off second base, the shortstop or the second baseman, whoever takes the throw, runs him hard toward third base. The pitcher immediately goes to third base, and the third baseman moves up the base line several yards. As the runner approaches the third baseman, the player making the play throws the ball, rotates to his right, and follows the throw. The third baseman should have time to tag the runner before he can change directions. If this play is executed properly, the runner should be put out in one throw. Some coaches do not like running the base runner hard away from the base from which he was picked off. If this be true, get the ball to the third baseman and let him run the base runner hard toward second base. The throw then will go to the shortstop or the second baseman, whoever is left, and the runner should be tagged out in two throws.

If a runner is caught off third base by the ball being hit to the pitcher, the pitcher should run directly toward him. This will make him commit himself, preferably toward third, and it is an easy matter to throw him out. The first baseman backs up the catcher at home plate, and the shortstop backs up the play at third base. As soon as the pitcher throws either to third or home, he backs up that base.

If the pitcher picks the runner off third, he should back up that base. The first baseman goes to home plate and the shortstop to third. The third baseman chases the runner several yards toward the plate and throws to the catcher, who runs full speed at him and throws to the shortstop for the put out. The shortstop should be several feet in front of third base and in a position to make the tag before the runner has time to change directions.

In the single rotation system only one player rotates, while the other players remain stationary. When the pitcher picks the runner off first base, he immediately backs up that base. The first baseman throws the ball to the second baseman and remains stationary. The shortstop backs up the second baseman. The second baseman runs hard toward the runner and throws the ball when the runner is in position to be tagged out by the first baseman. If necessary the second baseman rotates to the right. This play has the shortstop and the second baseman on one end and the first baseman on the other, while the pitcher backs up first.

If the runner is picked off second base, the shortstop and the second baseman handle second and rotate, while the third baseman remains stationary. The pitcher backs up third base.

If the runner is picked off third base, the shortstop goes to third. The third baseman rotates, and the catcher remain stationary. The pitcher goes where the throw is made, and the first baseman covers home with the catcher.

The important things to remember in all run-downs are to get the runner going full speed, throw the ball no more than two times, hold the ball up in a throwing position, and not let the runner make contact with a defensive infielder. It should be pointed out that if a runner breaks fast to the next base, the ball should be thrown immediately to that base. There is a growing trend among coaches toward eliminating any fakes on the part of the infielders involved. If a fake is used, it is recommended that only one full arm fake be made.

PICK-OFF PLAYS

Pick-off plays deserve considerable discussion, since they can be extremely effective in games in which the score is close. For a runner to fall victim to a well-executed pick-off play not only places him in an embarrassing position, but also erases his scoring potential. A team that makes use of a reservoir of applicable pick-off plays can accomplish the following: 1. Erase potential runs; 2. Force opposing runners to be honest; 3. Lessen the defensive pressure; 4. Enjoy a psychological advantage; 5. Create greater defensive alertness.

The plays that will be explained have been identified by names which best describe the action required and the base involved in the play. The coach may have a vocal signal with which to start the play or alert the player who has the responsibility of initiating it.

First-Base Pick-Off. Runners are on first and second base with fewer than two out and preferably a righthanded hitter at the plate. The first baseman or the catcher initiates the play with a pre-arranged signal.

The first baseman plays very deep. As the pitcher starts his delivery, the first baseman breaks directly at the runner and then turns sharply to the base. The catcher, who generally calls for a breaking pitch or a pitch-out away from the righthanded hitter, then makes the throw to first.

It is amazing how many first base coaches will watch the pitch to the plate, and therein lies the key to the success of the play.

Catcher's Choice at First. With a runner on first base and a sacrifice bunt situation anticipated, this play may work. It is called by the catcher. Upon receiving the signal, the pitcher will pitch wide, so the batter is unable to bunt the ball. As the pitcher goes into his stretch, the first baseman rushes in for the expected bunt. The second baseman leaves his position to take the throw at first. He should run to a point a few feet back of first base, so he may approach the bag parallel to the base line. In this position he is better able to shift his feet should the throw be wide, and he can make the tag more easily.

Back-Up Play at First. If a bunt is expected with a runner on first only and the pick-off signal is given, the first baseman takes several running steps toward the plate as the pitch is made, luring the runner a step or two from the base. Just before the ball reaches the batter, the first baseman whirls back to the base to receive the throw from the catcher. The same play can be used when a bunt is not expected, except the first baseman takes several running steps toward second base as the pitch is made and then hustles back to first just before the ball reaches the batter.

Pitcher-to-First Base. The runner on first base shows poor lead-off techniques by crossing the legs or dashing off the base at the wrong time. The first baseman gets the attention of the pitcher and calls the play. As the pitcher takes his stretch, he throws to first base while his arms are in the process of moving downward. Since most baserunners take their lead while the pitcher is stretching, the throw to first will catch the runner leaning toward second base.

The Jockey Pick-Off. When there is a runner on second base, the shortstop initiates the play by breaking two or three steps toward second base. The pitcher glances at the shortstop, who stops and then continues on to the base. The pitcher should whirl as the shortstop starts the second time. The throw should be timed so the ball and the shortstop reach the base at the same time. If the shortstop starts and then returns to his position, the pitcher glances at the second baseman, who has taken a few steps toward second and breaks for the base, when the runner begins to move toward third. If the second baseman does not break for the base, the pitcher delivers to the batter. The coach must make sure it is understood that there will be only one break to the base by each infielder. If the pitcher knows this, he will not pitch with either infielder out of position.

The Count Method. The shortstop gives the signal for this play, and the pitcher answers. The pitcher moves into the set position, and as his arms come to rest in front of his body, he starts counting—one, two, three, four. On the count of four, he whirls and throws to second base. The shortstop also starts counting when the pitcher comes to the set position and breaks for the base on two. Timing is very important on this play.

Pick at Second. This play is used when a runner on second is taking a long careless lead. The shortstop gives the signal to the pitcher and the second baseman. When the pitcher steps on the rubber, he turns his head toward the shortstop, who has gone wide and close to the hole, so the runner can see him and thus get off. In the meantime the second baseman has edged closer to second base. When the pitcher's foot contacts the rubber to take the stretch, the count begins. On the count of one the second baseman breaks, and on three the pitcher turns to throw for the pick-off.

Pick at Third. The play is used when a runner at third base is taking a long lead. The third baseman initiates the play by giving the signal to the pitcher. When the pitcher places his foot in contact with the rubber, the count begins. On the count of two the third baseman breaks for the bag, and on three the pitcher throws to third base. Since this is very dangerous play, the third baseman must be sure the baserunner is off far enough to be picked off. Timing is important, and this play will need several hours of practice.

It should be understood that a throw for a pick-off may be made anytime the batter misses the ball in an attempt to bunt or hit, if in the catcher's judgment a throw has merit. The runner usually takes an extra step as he sees the batter attempt to make contact with the ball. Therefore the infielders must hurry to their bases as soon as the ball passes the batter, ready for a throw from the catcher. A throw by the catcher or the pitcher should be knee high when the infielder receives it.

BASIC CUT-OFF AND RELAY PATTERNS

Basic cut-off plays are the backbone of good team defense. The importance of the cut-off man cannot be stressed too much. He must think quickly and diagnose plays instantly. When the opponents start running the bases, it is imperative for the defense to know exactly where to go and what to do. The defense cannot afford to make a mistake. Often a game is lost by a run that scored because a man advanced a base as a result of a poorly executed cut-off or relay play. Many of these mistakes result from erratic throwing on the part of the outfielders. They must understand that all throws toward the cut-off or the relay man should be low enough for him to handle. If a ball is hit between the outfielders, they can help each other by giving instructions, but they should never become the relay man.

Infielders should station themselves inside a base while watching the runner tag a base in making the turn. Their being inside the base has a tendency to make the runner take a wider turn, thus increasing the distance he travels toward the next base. The infielder must not interfere with the runner by being too close to the base.

On routine base hits and fly balls to the outfield with no one on base, the outfielders should form the habit of making *low, hard, one hop* throws to second base. The shortstop should cover on balls hit to left and center, while the second baseman covers on ball hit to right.

Some teams use the pitcher exclusively as their cut-off man. This is not a sound procedure because the pitcher is not an infielder. He does not take infield practice and consequently cannot field the ball as well as one who does. There is also the danger that he may injure his arm by throwing from an unnatural position.

Some high school teams, for simplicity, employ the first baseman exclusively as their cut-off man. This procedure is all right except when he is playing deep. From this position he cannot possibly get to the cut-off position on a sharp single to left field. Because of this problem, the system discussed here uses both the third and the first baseman as cut-off men. The third baseman is the cut-off man on a single to left field, on a fly ball to left with a man on third, or men on second and third. In all other situations, if there is a possible play at home, the first baseman acts as the cut-off man.

The objective of the defense in all the situations which will be diagrammed and explained is to have every base covered, every base backed up, and a player in the relay or cut-off positions whenever necessary. There are some situations on the double relay when extra-base hits will require leaving first base open. It is preferable to leave first open rather than any other base.

When an infielder acts as the cut-off man on throws from the outfield, he takes a position about 50 feet in front of the base to which the play is likely to be made, and in line with the throw. He should hold his arms in the air to give the outfielder a good target, and listen for the player covering the base to call "cut". No call means "let the ball go". If the throw is definitely too late to catch the runner, the cut-off man advances toward the ball so that he can intercept it sooner.

The shortstop and the second baseman act as relay men on very long fly balls that elude the outfielders. The shortstop performs this duty on balls to the left-field side and the second baseman on those to the right-field side. This is done at a point between 100 and 150 feet from the outfielder catching or retrieving the ball. The arms are above the head, and the infielder should be in line with the base to which the throw is to be made. In relaying the throw, the pivot should be executed toward the glove hand after the ball is caught.

Diagram 14-1. Single to Left Field, No One on Base.

Situation

1. Pitcher moves toward first base in case a play can be made there.
2. Catcher follows runner down line.
3. Shortstop covers second base.
4. Second baseman backs up the base.
5. Third baseman moves toward the mound for possible deflected ball.
6. The right fielder backs up the throw to second.

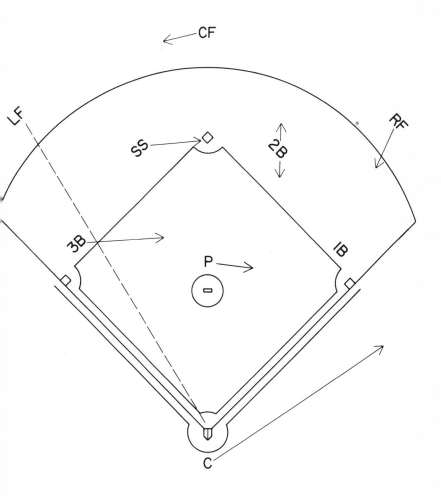

Diag. 14-1.

Diagram 14-2. Single to Center Field, No One on Base.

Situation
1. Pitcher backs up throw to second base.
2. Catcher follows runner down line.
3. Shortstop covers second base.
4. Second baseman backs up the base.
5. Third baseman moves toward second base for possible deflected ball.

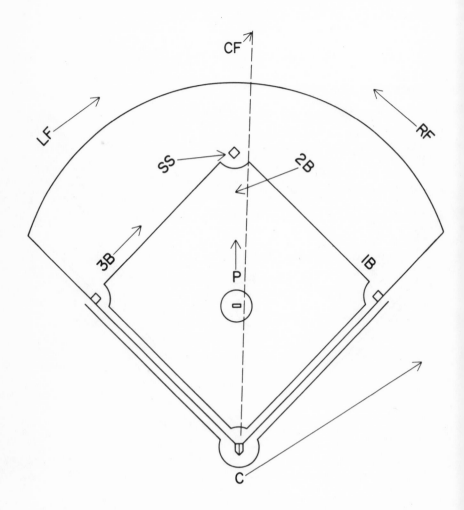

Diag. 14-2.

Diagram 14-3. Single to Right Field, No One on Base.

Situation

1. Pitcher moves to position half-way between second and third base.
2. Catcher follows runner down line.
3. Shortstop backs up the base.
4. Second baseman covers second base.
5. Third baseman backs up the play.
6. Leftfielder backs up the throw to second.

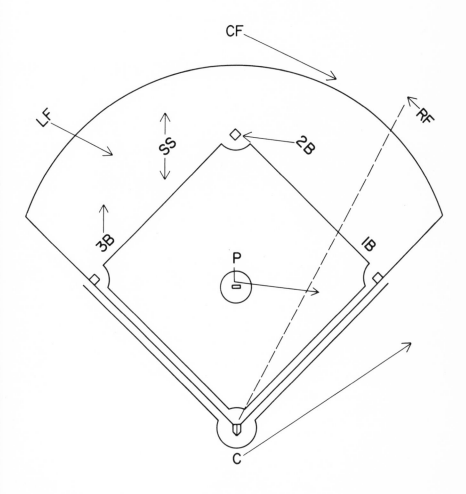

Diag. 14-3.

Diagram 14-4. Single to Right Field with First Base Occupied.

Situation

1. Pitcher backs up third base.
2. Catcher covers home plate.
3. Shortstop takes cutoff position in line with rightfielder and third base.
4. Second baseman covers second base.
5. Third baseman covers third base.
6. Leftfielder backs up throw to third base.

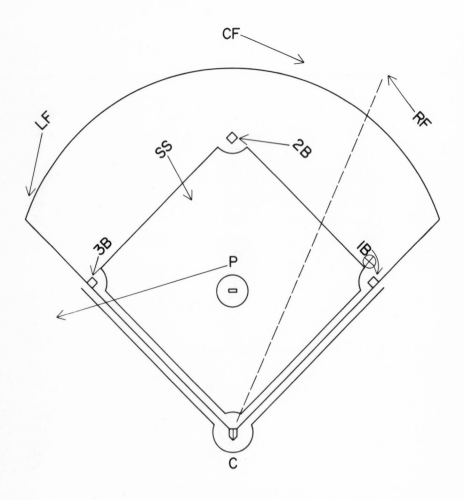

Diag. 14-4.

Diagram 14-5. Single to Center Field with First Base Occupied.

Situation

1. Pitcher backs up third base.
2. Shortstop takes cutoff position in line with centerfielder and third base.
3. Second baseman covers second.
4. Third baseman covers third.
5. First baseman covers first.

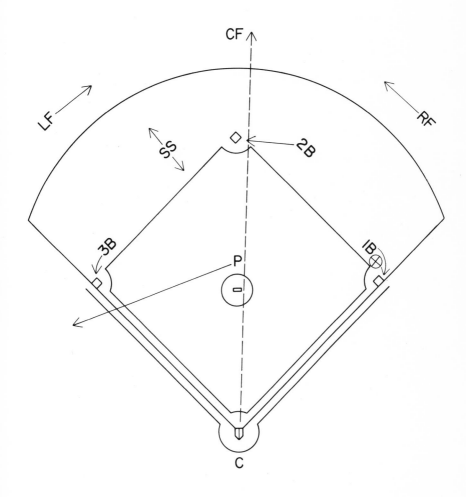

Diag. 14-5.

Diagram 14-6. Single to Left Field with First Base Occupied.

Situation
1. Pitcher backs up third base.
2. Catcher moves in behind the pitcher, to back up the play.
3. Shortstop takes cutoff position in line with leftfielder and third base.
4. Second baseman covers second.
5. Third baseman covers third.
6. Rightfielder backs up possible throw to second base.

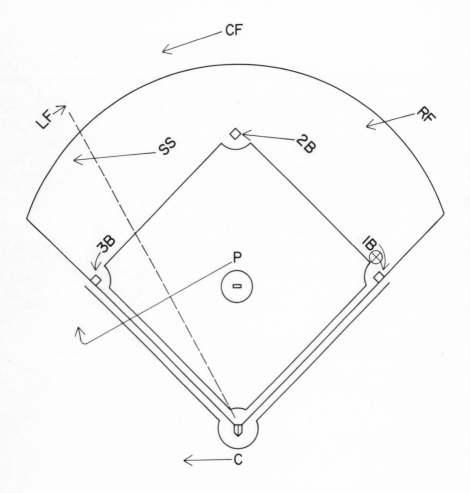

Diag. 14-6.

Diagram 14-7. Single to Right or Center Field with Second Base Occupied.

Situation
1. Pitcher backs up home plate.
2. Shortstop covers second.
3. Second baseman covers first.
4. First baseman lines up the throw to the plate.
5. Third baseman covers third.

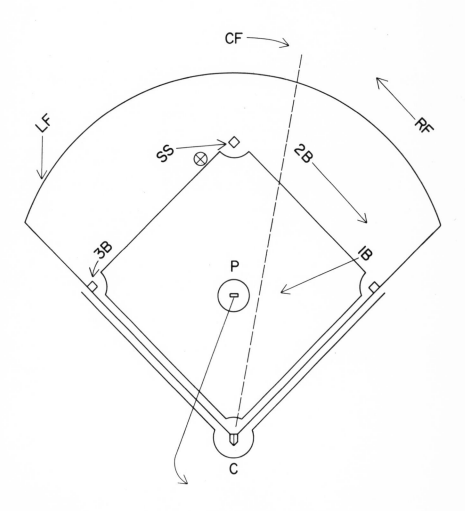

Diag. 14-7.

Diagram 14-8. Single to Left Field with Second Base Occupied.

Situation
1. Pitcher backs up home plate.
2. Shortstop covers third.
3. Second baseman covers second.
4. First baseman covers first.
5. Third baseman lines up the throw to the plate.

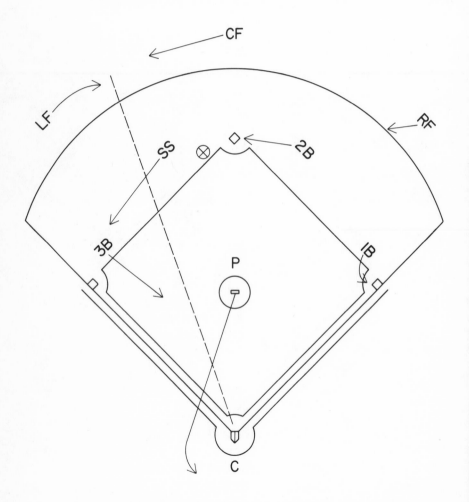

Diag. 14-8.

Diagram 14-9. Single to Right or Center Field with First and Second Occupied.

Situation

1. Pitcher breaks to a point halfway between home and third, sizing up the play and covering accordingly.
2. Shortstop lines up a possible throw to third from right or center field.
3. Second baseman covers second.
4. Third baseman covers third.
5. First baseman lines up possible throw to the plate. Score, inning, speed of ball hit, strength of outfielders, and speed of baserunners will determine where the ball will be thrown.

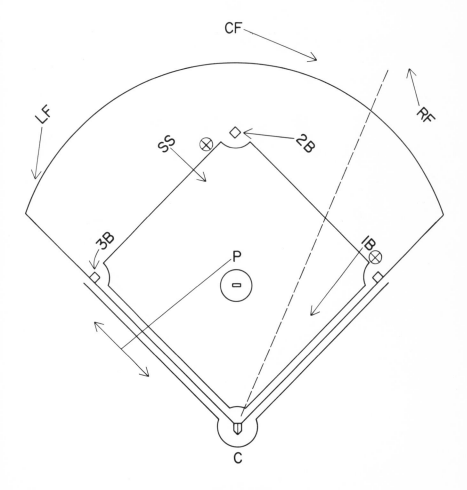

Diag. 14-9.

Diagram 14-10. Single to Left Field with First and Second Occupied.

Situation
1. Pitcher backs up the plate.
2. Shortstop covers third.
3. Second baseman covers second.
4. Third baseman lines up throw to plate.
5. First baseman covers first.

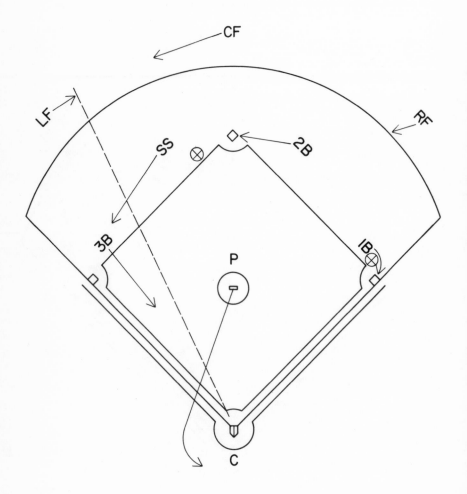

Diag. 14-10.

Diagram 14-11. Extra Base Hit to Right or Right Center Field with First Base Occupied.

Situation

1. Pitcher breaks to a point halfway between home and third, sizing up the play and covering accordingly.
2. Shortstop covers second and backs up the second baseman.
3. Second baseman acts as the relay man.
4. Third baseman covers third.
5. First baseman lines up the throw home.
6. Leftfielder backs up possible throw to second base.

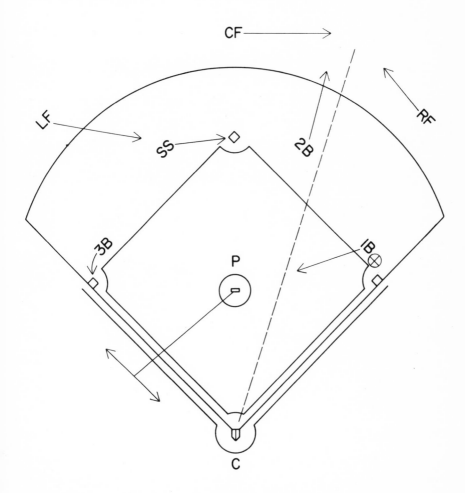

Diag. 14-11.

Diagram 14-12. Extra Base Hit to Left or Left Center Field with First Base Occupied.

Situation

1. Pitcher breaks to a point halfway between home and third, sizing up the play and covering accordingly.
2. Shortstop acts as the relay man.
3. Second baseman covers second and backs up the shortstop.
4. Third baseman covers third.
5. First baseman lines up the throw home.
6. Right fielder backs up possible throw to second base.

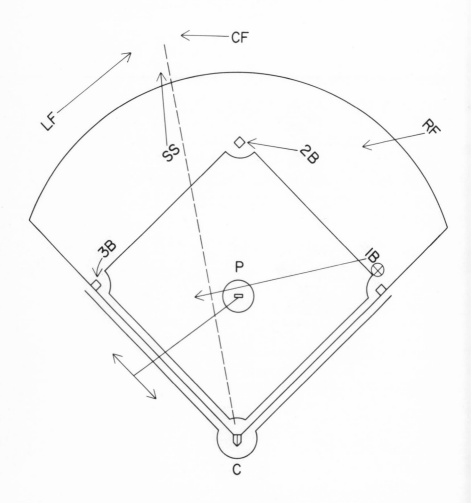

Diag. 14-12.

Diagram 14-13. Foul Fly Caught by Second Baseman, Runners on First and Third Base Are Tagging Up.

Situation
1. Pitcher backs up home plate.
2. Shortstop covers second.
3. Second baseman catches foul fly and throws to first baseman at once.
4. Third baseman covers third.
5. First baseman takes cutoff position about 20 feet from first base in line with home plate.
6. Centerfielder backs up second.
7. Leftfielder backs up third.

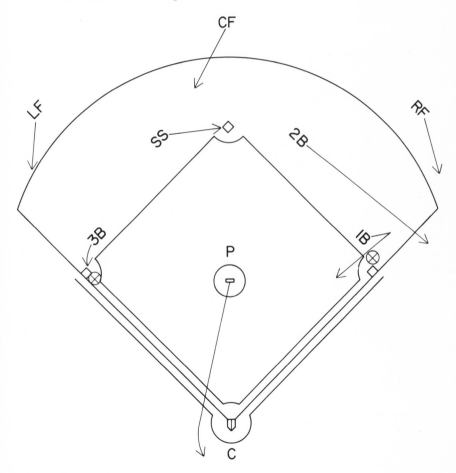

Diag. 14-13.

There are several variations which can be used in relay and cutoff positions, depending on personnel and the coach's philosophy of the game.

On a two-base hit with no one on base, or a possible three base hit, the shortstop, or the second baseman, depending on where the ball is hit, can act as the trailing relay man. The trailing relay man backs up the relay man at a distance of forty or fifty feet. In case the outfielder makes an erratic throw, the trailing relay man is in position to field the ball and keep the runner from taking an extra base. The first baseman trails the batter-runner and is in a position to cover second base if necessary.

If the third baseman has an exceptional arm, he may be used as the relay man on extra base hits to left field or left-center field. The shortstop would then cover third base.

BUNT SITUATIONS

Two bunt situations for which a team must perfect a defense are a runner on first base and runners on first and second base, with the bunt in order. There are other situations, but these two must be defensed, or the team will be in constant trouble.

When a runner is on first base with no one out, the third baseman should be alert for a possible bunt. The shortstop and the second baseman should play the double-play position, while the first baseman holds the runner on base. If the ball is bunted, the pitcher fields it if it is in front of him or to his left. The third baseman will field it if it is bunted to the pitcher's right and down the third base line. The catcher should field any bunt near home plate. If the pitcher or the third baseman fields the ball, the catcher should call the base to which the throw should be made. If the third baseman fields the ball, the catcher or the pitcher should cover third base. Some teams let the third baseman sprint back to third after fielding the ball to prevent the runner from first base going to third. But this is a difficult play for the third baseman, since he is moving away from the base when he fields the ball. If the pitcher or the catcher fields the bunt, the third baseman has adequate time to cover his base. The outfielders should back up the bases in case of a bad throw.

When runners are on first and second base with one or no outs and the situation calls for a bunt, the first and the third baseman play in. The shortstop and the second baseman can play at the double play position, but the second baseman must be sure he can cover first base. The pitcher must field the ball if bunted to his right, since the third baseman covers third base. The first baseman charges in and fields the ball if bunted on the first base side of the mound.

The second baseman covers first base, and the shortstop covers second. If the ball is bunted sharply down the third base side, the third baseman should field the ball and make the play to first. He should not charge forward until he sees the ball will get by the pitcher (Diag. 14-14). The pitcher should let the third baseman know when he is able to field the bunt. If he does not do this, the third baseman may charge the ball too quickly, and no one will be covering third if the pitcher fields the bunted ball.

When the pitcher takes his stretch, he should watch the shortstop and deliver the ball when the shortstop fakes the runner back into second base. This prevents the runner from getting a big lead and makes possible the force play at third base. If the runner takes a long lead, the pitcher should throw to the shortstop as he covers the base.

Here is a play used at Lipscomb with runners on first and second base, no outs, and a close score in a late inning, when the defensive

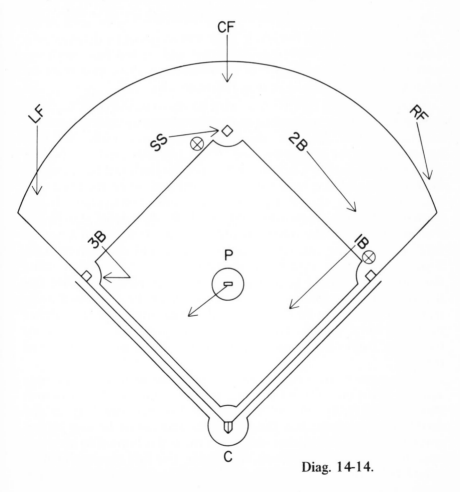

Diag. 14-14.

team cannot allow the offense to move a runner to third. The first and the third baseman play in. The shortstop and the second baseman play close to the base at second. The play is called by the coach, and all infielders must know when it is to be executed. As the pitcher comes to his set position, he is looking toward second base. When he turns his head toward home plate, the shortstop sprints to third base and the second baseman breaks for second. The pitcher turns his head back toward second, and if the runner has moved off the base, he turns and throws to it. If the second baseman's movement toward the base has caused the runner to shorten his lead, the pitcher throws the batter a waist high fast ball, directly over the middle of the plate. On the delivery to the batter, the first baseman and the third baseman charge as fast as they can and still maintain body balance. The player fielding the ball will throw to the shortstop covering third base (Diag. 14-15). It is important for the third

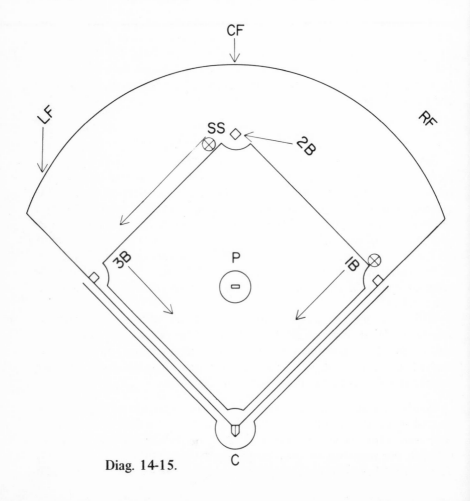

Diag. 14-15.

baseman to wait for the pitcher's delivery before he charges toward the plate. Some base runners will try to outrun the shortstop to third base. If this happens, the pitcher can back off the rubber and throw to the third baseman, who can retreat several yards to cover the base.

When the squeeze play has been detected, the pitcher should throw a fast ball inside and at the hips of a righthanded batter. This is a very difficult pitch to bunt. It is the job of the pitcher to throw an unbuntable pitch but one the catcher can handle. If the catcher is sure the squeeze play is on, he may call for a pitch-out. If the batter is left-handed, the pitcher should throw outside, so he will have to step over home plate to reach it. Then the batter should be called out and the runner returned to third base.

The catcher and the pitcher should remember that regardless of the pitch which may have been called, when the squeeze play breaks, it automatically is changed to a fast ball.

The pitcher is the key player in breaking up the squeeze. The pitch delivered to the batter will determine to a large degree if the play succeeds or fails. The third baseman can help by alerting the pitcher when the runner leaves, and the catcher can help by reacting to the situation, but the only person who can break up the play is the pitcher.

DEFENSIVE STEAL SITUATIONS

Single Steal. When a runner is on first base, the catcher must be alert at all times for a possible steal. In a steal situation he may call for a pitch-out and try to pick off the runner at first or throw him out at second. If the runner should break from first base before the pitcher begins his delivery, he should step backward off the rubber and throw to the player covering second. The first baseman should be ready at all times to take a pick-off throw from either the pitcher or the catcher, while the player designated to cover second base must constantly watch the runner and be ready to receive a throw from the catcher.

With a runner on second base, the catcher should anticipate an attempted steal of third. In this situation, he may throw the runner out at third or trap him off second on a pitch-out. If he breaks toward third base, the pitcher should quickly step back off the rubber and throw to the third baseman covering.

Double Steal. In most cases, the batter determines whether the shortstop or the second baseman will cover on a double steal with first and third bases occupied. Usually it is the second baseman, because the majority of players are righthanded and hit to left field. The second baseman is the logical player to cover, since his approach to the base enables him to watch the runner on third. If the second baseman does not have a strong arm, it is preferable for the shortstop to take the throw. When covering the base in this situation, the infielder should make an attempt to reach the front of it, since this is the best position from which to run in on the ball should the runner on third start for the plate. If the runner on third shows no intentions of leaving that base, an attempt is made to tag the runner coming from first. If the runner approaching second base stops, the infielders start a run-down, while watching the runner on third, since most players attempt to break for the plate during the process of the run-down.

Some coaches prefer to defense the first and third situation by having one player cover and the other player stand 15 or 20 feet in front of the base in line with the throw (Diag. 14-16). This permits the player in the short position to intercept the throw if the runner

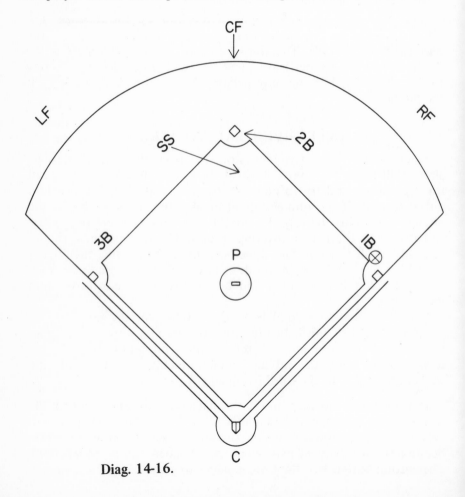

Diag. 14-16.

on third base attempts to score, or allows the throw to go through to the player covering second, should the runner remain at third. This method of covering the play requires either the shortstop or the second baseman to play out of position in order to reach this station in time for the throw, unless all batters are played to hit straight-away. However, this position may be necessary if neither the shortstop nor the second baseman has the arm to make the play from the base.

A clever catcher who "looks" the runner back at third and infielders with strong arms will almost always prevent the offensive team from scoring under these circumstances. If the defensive team holds a commanding lead, the runner at third is disregarded. The game situation will always determine the strategy used concerning the runner at third. If he is the winning run, the fake to third is made, and the catcher throws back to the pitcher.

Delayed Steal. Occasionally a team will attempt a delayed steal. The runner on first may go all the way to second or stop halfway, with the intention of letting himself be trapped, so the man on third can score. The player who has the responsibility of covering second base should move several steps toward second after the ball has passed the batter, thus insuring that it will be covered if the runner does go all the way. When the runner leaves first, the first baseman should move down the line with him, so that in case he does stop halfway, the infielder covering at second can quickly relay the ball to the first baseman, who makes the tag and runs the ball in to prevent the runner on third from scoring.

THE INTENTIONAL PASS

An intentional pass frequently is used as defensive strategy late in the game with second base or second and third bases occupied and fewer than two out. If the batter is the tying or winning run, it is not sound strategy to pass him intentionally.

Some coaches who have a lefthanded pitcher on the mound will intentionally pass a right-handed batter to pitch to a left-handed hitter, if runners are in scoring position and first base is open. The intentional pass may be employed after a batter hits a double with the score tied and none out in the late inning. This creates a force-play situation at third base if the batter bunts and a double play situation if he hits away. If the first batter hits a triple in the last half of the last inning, the coach may issue two passes so that a force play is possible at the plate.

The coach usually has the responsibility of deciding when an intentional pass will be issued. He may give this information by pointing to first base or using some vocal signal.

INDEX

46778

DATE DUE

NOV 13 74			
APR 15 '76			
FEB 11 '77			
GAYLORD			PRINTED IN U.S.A